ROMANESQUE ART

IN FRANCE

ROMANESQUE ART IN FRANCE

JOSEPH GANTNER AND MARCEL POBÉ

WITH A PREFACE BY

MARCEL AUBERT

271 PICTURES IN PHOTOGRAVURE

BY JEAN ROUBIER

AND 8 MAPS

THAMES AND HUDSON

TRANSLATED FROM THE GERMAN BY

MARIE HEYNEMANN

1956

TEXT PRINTED IN GREAT BRITAIN BY JARROLD AND SONS LTD NORWICH
GRAVURE PLATES PRINTED IN FRANCE BY ETS BRAUN ET CIE MULHOUSE

PREFACE

THIS book deals with Romanesque art in France. It is the work of Professor Joseph Gantner, Head of the Institute of Art History at Basle University. Among many other activities he is editing the great History of Swiss Art, of which he has written the first two volumes himself. His collaborator is Dr Marcel Pobé, former lecturer in the faculty of philosophy at the University of Fribourg. His family comes from Lorraine and has settled in Switzerland. He specializes in the study of French civilization, especially the cultural history and art of Provence. The superb plates comprise 271 mainly full-page reproductions of photographs by Jean Roubier, who like a true artist has infused new life into the documentary study of the art of the Middle Ages now placed at the disposal of the archaeologist.

In a comprehensive account of the conditions of civilization in France in the eleventh and twelfth centuries Marcel Pobé shows how, after the chaos of the tenth century—famine, a reign of terror and all the horrors of the Norman and Hungarian invasions—literature and art gradually re-emerged. This rebirth took place in the great abbeys, the centres of the pilgrims' routes, in the collegiate churches protected by the stone fortifications and towers which rise everywhere in France; these are spread far and wide in feudal fiefs which grew up round the young Capetian monarchy then arising on the ruins of the Carolingian empire. These feudal states included the dukedoms of Normandy, Aquitaine, Gascony and Burgundy, the counties of Flanders, Champagne, Anjou and Brittany, of Toulouse and the Rouergue. Here Romanesque art flourished in the eleventh century and in the first half of the twelfth century as a visible emblem of a renaissance which, thanks to the courage and power of Otto the Great of the Saxon dynasty, the member states of the German empire had already experienced half a century before. Here were erected the splendid buildings whose vast dimensions and rich embellishment roused the admiration and sometimes also the anger of certain moralists of the period.

Romanesque art attracts and impresses us even today. It attracts us by its vigour, its abundance, its massive structure, the thickness of its walls, its perfect adaptation to the country, the climate and the soil in which it is firmly rooted, the manner in which it fulfils the purpose for which it was planned, the nobility of its design, the impetus of its final achievement. It impresses us by the mystery of its shadowy masses and even more by its decoration. If the eleventh century is the time of experiment, and sometimes also of accomplishment, the twelfth century is the age of the heroic epics, of the poetry of the courts, of the flourishing of schools, and its monuments are worthy of this greatness, of this epic enthusiasm.

The instruction given in its iconography has at the same time a religious, historic, didactic and moral character. The scenes represented always have a hidden symbolic or allegoric meaning. The significance of the animals, the fabulous beings, the monsters taken from the cultural heritage of all nations, even the plant motifs, derive their significance primarily from what they represent as symbols of historical, religious and moral truths; even the numbers have their own beauty, their special symbolic meaning.

The sculpture is plastic ornament and as such is incorporated in the building. Displayed like a tapestry on the bare wall, it adapts itself exactly to the shape of the given frame. Filled with an overflowing life, it can take any dimension and can fit each complex surface of the framework. Thus the story of Christ is represented in a dramatic style easy to apprehend; the vision of the Apocalypse, the miracles of the saints, the struggles of men against monsters and the powers of hell, horrible or fantastic shapes engendered by the imagination of visionaries, or drawn from the most authentic bestiaries of the farthest East—all are deployed on huge walls from whose roughly hewn shadowy recesses the figures seem to stand out, still further emphasized by their colours, so that we are to some extent reminded of the frescoes and mosaics of earlier basilicas.

Joseph Gantner's interpretation of this is based on his wide knowledge of French monuments —he has already published an excellent and highly successful work on Romanesque plastic art. Drawing from the best authors and from his own observation, he here sums up all that is known of architecture, sculpture and painting of the Romanesque period.

Jean Roubier's beautiful photographs are arranged topographically and to peruse them is like making a real journey through the whole of Romanesque France. He takes us by way of Burgundy, Provence and the valley of the Rhône from Vienne to Saintes-Maries-de-la-Mer; to Languedoc and the country of the Pyrenees from Roussillon to Béarn; to the Massif Central from Moissac as far as Le Puy, Auvergne and Berry; through the Limousin into Poitou, Saintonge and Aquitaine. From Anjou we pass through the valleys of the Loire and its tributaries to the Ile-de-France and the royal domain; then we travel through Normandy and Maine; finally, the circular tour ends in the eastern districts of Alsace and Lorraine. It is a marvellous journey, which we can make without leaving our homes; a journey, however, which will awaken the desire to know and see with our own eyes all these churches, sculptures and paintings. The admirable texts by Joseph Gantner and Marcel Pobé throw light upon the grandeur and variety of these Romanesque monuments and at the same time show how they fulfil the ever-present desire to erect solid, massive, vaulted and well-lit buildings. At the same time we recognize in what manifold ways the problems inherent in such a programme were solved, how the spatial structure was organized, how the masses were balanced, how the sculptural decoration was used inside and outside, how vast bare walls were reserved for paintings whose beauty is not inferior to the historical and mystic interest of the figures represented.

All these monuments bear the stamp of original creative genius, whose vigorous breath was felt far beyond the frontiers of France, in England, in the Germanic countries, in Italy; it reached Spain with the Reconquista, and the crusaders carried it as far as the Orient. Everywhere the personality of the artist, the architect, the sculptor and the painter is beginning to emerge in the service of a transcendental idea which is greater than he, and which in its symbolic content attains a value that is eternal.

MARCEL AUBERT
Member of the "Institut de France"

JOSEPH GANTNER

ROMANESQUE ART IN FRANCE

I

AMONG all the great styles known to the history of European art the Romanesque was the last to receive public recognition. The generation which experienced that tremendous "rebirth" which has come to be known as the Renaissance itself already spoke of the revival of a more ancient language of forms, and it is well known that at that time the phenomenon of Gothic art was recognized as a style—though with an underlying rejection and condemnation. And it was exactly the same with the Baroque style. This style was determined by protest against it, having been formulated by men of the late eighteenth century who indignantly defined as "Baroque" the style that was just going out of fashion.

If the men of the twelfth century had cared to define and characterize the phenomenon which nowadays we call Romanesque, their definition might well have been found in the protest of Bernard of Clairvaux. However, the first great experience of this art was granted to the generation of the French Romantics.

In a now famous letter of December 1818 the Norman archaeologist de Gerville speaks of an "architecture lourde et grossière", of an "*opus romanum* dénaturé ou successivement dégradé par nos rudes ancêtres". Over this first characterization still hovers the shadow of the classical aesthetic from which, as much as a hundred years later, even the great master Emile Mâle could not quite dissociate himself. Nonetheless, it seems as though with the name some interpretation of the mystery of the style had been found, and the lovers of art who, in 1834, formed the "Société Française d'Archéologie" began to look with greater attention at the strange forms which witnessed to a past as mysterious as it was monumental. The notable report which the writer Prosper Mérimée, who was then Inspector of Ancient Monuments, sent to his Minister on the mural paintings of Saint-Savin (Plates 181–186) already displays genuine enthusiasm.

What then is the inner relationship between the sentiments of the Romantics and the forms of Romanesque art? The plates illustrating this book, especially those showing the capitals and the paintings give a clear answer. It was the supernatural, irrational world which impressed the Romantic, a world based on the idea of unconditional devotion to God. This world opened up quite new vistas, and revealed the dream-like as well as the grotesque, the strong and cruel as well as the gentle and delicate. It was those very aspects of Romanesque art which 700 years earlier Bernard of Clairvaux, the passionate contemporary, had censured as *"ridicula monstruositas"*, *"deformis formositas"*—that especially delighted the eyes and rejoiced the heart of the Romantic who—according to Baudelaire—liked to take refuge from the "trivialité positive" in the "monstres de la fantaisie".

Yet the history of Romanesque art-research during the nineteenth century proves that this first flowering of interest in the circle of the Romantics would not have sufficed to give Romanesque art that commanding position which it occupies in the twentieth century. To achieve this the field had to be ploughed once more, and this tillage we owe to the abstract art of the age in which we live.

Through the present-day tendency in art to dematerialize the subject, we are enabled to look deeper into both the hidden and the manifest abstractions of Romanesque art, to recognize better its effects on the entire language of artistic form, and to distinguish these effects in their individual, yet manifold degrees. Of course, Romanesque art aspires no more than any other historic style to that total abstraction which makes modern art such an unique phenomenon in the history of the human mind. On the contrary, it is completely dominated by its subject matter. But since, with an exclusiveness that was never to occur again, this subject matter is God alone—that is, a spiritual power in the highest sense—the shaping of Romanesque art is by its very nature lodged in the sphere of pure imagination, and it is this that brings it so close to our modern sensibilities. For, far removed as it is from all traditional religious feeling, this modern outlook has created in its own way a world of pure symbols.

When we read what the most important investigators of Romanesque art have written, we recognize how slowly and with how much difficulty this insight was won. Confronted by the tympanum of Saint-Lazare at Autun (Plate 20) Emile Mâle still speaks of an "incorrection farouche" in the representation of the figures, while at the same time Max Dvořák calls the portal figures of Bourges repulsive and cadaverous. Even Henri Focillon, whose work on French Romanesque art represents the first really scientific and profound analysis of this style, when confronted by Romanesque works of art, poses the anxious—although perhaps no more than rhetorical—question: "Un tel abîme, dans la conception du monde, de l'homme et de la vie, nous sépare-t-il de nos ancêtres?"

At the same time French scholars, notably Marcel Aubert and Paul Deschamps, did a great deal of admirable work remarkable in its scope, on the French Romanesque heritage. Without these studies, which take the whole of France into account, our survey would be quite impossible.

It was Henri Focillon who gave the Romanesque style its place in the history of European art by stating that "la première définition de l'Occident" had become manifest in it. If to such a formulation we add that of all the comparable countries of this "Occident" none can show such a wealth of magnificent examples of Romanesque monuments as France, the importance of our theme is clear.

"La première définition de l'Occident"—in view of the sudden renewal of our knowledge of pre-Romanesque art, resulting from the new discoveries which have been made all over Europe in the last twenty years, we may well ask the question whether Romanesque art should be granted this high status. However, we need only consider France to see that it is still justified. Nowhere else do the monuments of earlier centuries appear in such almost uninterrupted unity of style, and the beautiful words of the monk Glaber to the effect that shortly after the year 1000 all the world—but especially France and Italy—was covered with a white garment of churches, would not have been true of any earlier epoch. Surely the monk of Cluny pronounced these words with such emphasis because this particular phenomenon represented something new, extraordinary, unprecedented.

Great spiritual movements which change the face of the world cannot be compressed into definite periods of time. They often have their roots and their sources in remote ages, and their influence endures far beyond their actual life. But what is important is their period of flowering: those works in which the vigour of the artistic expression flows purely and without hindrance.

In this sense the year 1000 really marks the beginning of great Romanesque art. Did we wish to compare the moving words of the monk Glaber with a document revealing with like insight the end of a style and the beginning of a new situation, we should choose the record of Abbot Suger of Saint-Denis, written about 1148–9, which clearly reflects how the position had changed. The great period of Romanesque art in France is from 1000 to 1150, and most of the monuments illustrated in this volume date from that time. The fact that some of them had already been erected in the tenth century, and others—especially those in the south—not until towards the end of the twelfth century, strengthens the impression of monumental unity which characterizes this flowering of Romanesque art.

We cannot deal here with the question of the inner development of the style and shall only mention the much disputed problems of the "Romanesque Schools" where these are readily recognizable in buildings and sculpture. Throughout the vast number of schools and regions in France, whose boundaries are, in any case, perpetually subject to change, we have the wider influence of the Monastic Orders and the pilgrims' routes which imposed themselves in varying degrees on the prevailing stylistic language.

The picture thus revealed, the wonderful picture of an art evenly diffused over a whole country, would be still richer and grander, had not, as early as the middle of the twelfth century,

Gothic art violently overthrown Romanesque art, and, in an unparalleled triumphal march spread its new canon over the whole of northern and central France. Wherever we find Gothic cathedrals in towns in the Ile-de-France, in Champagne, in Picardy, even in the Loire valley, we know that this new splendour had to be purchased at a high price, with the destruction of Romanesque or Carolingian buildings and sculpture. In our volume a single illustration suffices to represent Romanesque Paris (Plate 234), and though the surviving monuments are in fact more numerous, every visitor to this incomparable city knows that her Romanesque art has been irrevocably lost. The miraculously preserved west front of Chartres (Plates 216–220) shows us with almost overwhelming clarity what treasures were destroyed, as do the group, recently discovered, of delicately carved capitals in the chapter-house of Saint-Rémi at Reims (Plates 243–246).

In no other style of the post-classical centuries does the monumental ruin play such an important part in the appearance of still extant buildings. The pre-Romanesque art of the first millennium is now an art of scattered fragments. In the post-Romanesque period, especially in Gothic art, we find grandiose ruins, justifiably beloved by the Romantic painters—even invented by them as fantastic creations. But the really great ruin which in its worn and weathered form still gives us an idea of its vanished beauty, which offers a lasting stimulation to our imaginative faculty—and that is the most fundamental attribute of the style—such a ruin is to be found above all in Romanesque art. And the country which shows us the greatest number of monuments also shows us the greatest number of ruins.

It matters little what the outward causes of the destruction may have been—natural decay, secularization after the wars of religion, savage pillaging during the Revolution which spared nothing—the vandals nearly always destroyed important, representative works whose fragments now confront us like a petrified lament. Saint-Martin at Tours, says Emile Mâle, was as important to ancient France as the Temple of Delphi to ancient Greece—nothing but a small fragment of the church remains. The third church of Cluny, a miracle of grandeur and artistic detail, was attacked by Bernard de Clairvaux with the passion of the zealot who secretly admires. Fragments of the transept, the choir and the capitals alone survive to give a faint idea of the magical and serene dignity once possessed by this, the greatest church of the West (Plate 15). The rotundas of Dijon and Charroux (Plate 175), the ruins of La Charité-sur-Loire (Plate 43) and of the abbey-church of Jumièges (Plate 256), the fragments on Mont Saint-Michel (Plates 247, 248) and of Saint-Gilles (Plates 94–96)—as well as many other smaller buildings, among which Charlieu (Plates 57–60) awakens a deep feeling of nostalgia—bear eloquent testimony to the irreparable losses which Romanesque art has suffered. One might be tempted to say that by this destruction the history of the cathedral in France has been deprived of its first chapter—that recording those grand basilicas of the eleventh century in which the architectural idea of the cathedral was expressed for the first time. How fortunate it is that numerous other buildings testifying to this heroic conception have been preserved! Saint-Savin (Plate 181), Saint-Benoît-sur-Loire (Plates 224–230), Conques (Plates 134–136), Périgueux (Plates 187, 188), the two churches at Caen (Plates 249, 252) and above all the majestic church of Saint-Sernin at Toulouse (Plate 99) which, according to our present knowledge, shows the type of these early cathedrals at its purest. Indeed, in this same Toulouse the Musée des Augustins preserves the most important remnants of Romanesque sculpture in France: the fragments of statues and capitals from three of the town's destroyed cloisters (Plates 102–106) forming a repertory of plastic forms and artistic creative power of incomparable wealth.

II

How can the present-day observer classify this great heritage?

Our survey which, as is only logical, gives first place to architecture, must begin here, too, by drawing attention to a gap. The over-all aspect of the Romanesque town is nowhere clear enough to enable us to recognize it with perfect accuracy as an organic whole. The few remaining fragments of Romanesque secular buildings, of which we illustrate a house at Saint-Antonin (Plate 107) and above all the numerous portions of Romanesque monasteries (Plates 31, 60, 98, 112, 166, 247, 257) teach us that in the construction of even those very small groups of buildings Roman order and reason were still apparent. And Romanesque castles and bridges (Plates 87, 233) bear similar testimony. Judging by their ground-plans and by the dimensions of their walls, arches and vaults, all these buildings were developed from the simple forms of the square, the circle or the semicircle in which—to quote a beautiful saying of Leonardo's—"tutto il travagliamento delle superfizie geometriche" finds tranquillity. Therefore they retain an inner calm and monumentality which move us even in their fragments.

Especially magical in effect must have been the humblest part of that "*candida ecclesiarum vestis*", which after the year 1000 invested the small towns, villages and hamlets of Fance, even the most isolated hermitages and leper-houses, of which our illustrations give some beautiful examples (Plates 39, 64, 71, 77, 84, 148, 189, 198, 254). What a wealth of individual forms! As if in each case a new imagination, another artist's hand had been at work, the various parts of the buildings are associated and combined in ever fresh groupings. The nave alone, and sometimes the choir, can be regarded as essential to their cubical appearance. The transept is already a dispensable addition, and both the position and number of the towers vary. As though the idea of impairing the effect of the portals, which were generally decorated with sculpture, was displeasing, porches at the entrances were comparatively rare. Moreover, a western apse such as that of the magnificently situated church of La Garde-Adhémar (Plate 70) is an exception.

We know from the polemic treatise of Bernard of Clairvaux—and the monuments confirm it step by step—that it was not until the late phase of Romanesque art that a fundamental difference between the parish churches of the towns and the monastic churches of the countryside could be recognized. Of particular authority is the example of Caen, where the two great abbey churches, La Trinité and Saint-Etienne (Plates 249, 252) unite all the monumental qualities of the Romanesque style, and the parish church of Saint-Nicolas (Plate 253) appears insignificant beside them. As the clergy of the town churches were organized along monastic lines their requirements remained with few minor exceptions the same, so that the type of building that was to be decisive for the entire period was certainly the one which had gradually evolved during the Carolingian age: a nave with two aisles, a transept and an eastern limb, which as early as the tenth century was raised to greater importance by the addition of an ambulatory and radiating chapels. We should be justified in naming this type "Benedictine-Cluniac", for it dominates French Romanesque art, and the greatest and most beautiful churches of the country follow its pattern. It has its origin in the Benedictine abbey-church, which provided the dominating pattern in Carolingian times, and from the tenth century on benefited by the advances in spatial conception as well as by the refinements of detail which Cluniac reform of ecclesiastical architecture spread so quickly even beyond its own Order. We should mention here, *en passant*, that even the oldest churches of the Cistercian Order in the south caught a last reflection of this grand architecture (Plate 76)—although, at a very early stage, they resolutely abandoned it in order to develop a number of specifically Gothic elements.

This Benedictine-Cluniac type of abbey-church, which our volume illustrates in a wide variety of examples, is the key to the Romanesque art of France and therefore also the central repository of sculpture and painting. It is of surprising diversity, as are the smaller churches of the towns and villages. It varies from district to district. The Burgundian abbey-church differs completely from that of the Auvergne or Languedoc, the abbey-church of Poitou differs from that of Normandy. And each of these "schools" allows so many deviations from the norm, that in many cases the norm itself is challenged and the wealth of solutions outshines all rules.

For a long time scholars took it for granted that this unity of type was broken in the first place by certain great churches which, situated on the pilgrims' route to Santiago de Compostella, imitated the ground-plan of this pre-eminent church of pilgrimage. Our plates show two churches from this glorious group: Saint-Sernin at Toulouse (Plates 99, 101) and Sainte-Foy at Conques (Plates 134, 136). What connects these churches with Compostella and the destroyed buildings of Saint-Martin at Tours and Saint-Martial at Limoges is the vast space occupied by the whole structure, which is clearly meant to accommodate large numbers of pilgrims. For the same reason, the choir and the transept are considerably enlarged; at Toulouse and at Conques as at Compostella and at Tours the transept has aisles—an earnest of what was to be a very important element of the later Gothic cathedral. None of the other parts of the church, including the architectural detail and the sculptural and painted decoration, acquire any special "pilgrim-route" character, but make full use of the artistic forms of their own district. Scholars have long recognized that the church of Saint-Martin at Tours has a prime significance among these pilgrim-churches.

On the other hand, those strange domed churches, which appear as simple halls with or without transept as at Angoulême (Plate 190) or as a huge central rotunda with five cupolas as at Saint-Front in Périgueux (Plates 187, 188), still pose a serious problem to scholars. How are we to interpret within the field of Romanesque art this "Byzantine" influence which invests the quiet landscape of old Aquitaine with such a strange Oriental flavour?

Our text has neither the pretension nor the space to explore these architectural peculiarities. However, we are confronted here with a problem so specifically Romanesque and so specifically French that we would like to hint at a possible explanation. The wide domes may be explained by the survival of Roman architecture clearly in evidence at Périgueux, by the fragments of antique rotundas whose system of vaulting may have been transferred to the naves of the great Romanesque churches, just as the construction of the Roman city gates was applied to the triforium of Saint-Lazare at Autun (Plate 24). And the five cupolas of Saint-Front may have been modelled on the Church of the Apostles at Constantinople, which has only recently been recognized as the architectural prototype for the first lay-out of St Mark's in Venice (*ca.* 830), long before Saint-Front was built.

Thus to the relatively small, early Romanesque "Latin" Basilica of Périgueux, whose façade is still preserved as an entrance porch and serves as a casing for the large, lavishly articulated tower that was erected much later, was added a copy of the Church of the Apostles to constitute a huge "Byzantine" dome-structure. The same process, moreover, took place in numerous other Romanesque basilicas which aimed at an ideal imitation of the Church of the Holy Sepulchre at Jerusalem with its great domed choir. The most famous examples are Saint-Bénigne at Dijon and Charroux (Plate 175), two of the finest of their kind in France. The fact that as monumental centralized buildings their architectural type can be associated with the smaller centralized buildings of baptismal chapels and the churches of the Knight-Templars (Plates 75, 142, 148, 241) makes their appearance still more imposing.

In this exceedingly multiform organism the no less multiform creations of sculpture and painting developed. They are so intimately connected with the architecture which supports and encloses them, that time and again the question has been asked whether architecture did not actually impose its own laws on their forms. No doubt there are cases where the plastic form in particular appears to be a function of architecture, as for instance when on the capital of a pillar the supporting function of the block is emphasized in the figures (Mars-sur-Allier, Plates 158, 160).

However, we should be straining the truth and above all showing unawareness of the grand, inner freedom of this art, were we to see nothing more than the law of architecture realized in all the sculptured figures.

The artist's tasks, where the French Romanesque church is concerned, could be divided into five different groups:

1. The plastic ornament of the entrance, that is to say in the porticoes, on the walls of the façade and, particularly, in the porches.
2. The carved ornamentation of pillars and supports in the church itself, as well as in the cloisters—an exceedingly rich group, which is as yet by no means sufficiently recognized in all its wealth, and which culminates in the often bewitching beauty of the capitals.
3. The paintings on the walls and on the vaults, naturally preserved in much smaller numbers than the sculpture, but showing, by way of compensation, an enchanting freedom of style both in their iconography and in their execution. The fragments of stained glass and tapestry which have been preserved obviously also belong to this group.
4. The plastic and painted ornamentation of the altars, baptismal fonts and tombs, to which must be added the carved wooden cult images and the costly altar plate.
5. The illuminated manuscripts which played such an important rôle in spreading artistic motifs from district to district, even from country to country.

It is not our intention in the present work to describe such specialized items as stained glass and wooden images. In imposing this restriction, we are fully aware that the designs of such works are richly mirrored in the related monumental forms.

Of the above-mentioned five groups, the portals, capitals and wall-paintings are particularly impressive, but as they are profusely illustrated here, they shall be mentioned only briefly.

According to J. G. Burckhardt the repetition of kindred things in every kind of art gives particular pleasure. It seems that the same problem, ever posed anew, stimulates the artist's imagination to the highest achievements. Here it is as if Christ's solemn binding words: "*Ego sum janua vitae*" served as a perpetual inspiration, with the result that in the short period of two generations, from about 1090 to 1150, the Romanesque church portal in France blossomed into a beautiful maturity, as dozens of extant examples testify. Yet it is sad to think that that which is preserved forms only a fragment of what once existed. These portals in the "high" Romanesque style emerge from a preparatory period, during the eleventh century, in which isolated tympana, reliefs and figures in niches were created (Plates 82, 110, 138, 140, 194, 210, 265). They find their last great expression in the west porch of Chartres (Plates 216–220), then gradually dwindle in two widely divergent groups, which reflect the slowly changing conditions of a later period:

the late Romanesque porches of Provence (Plate 94) and the early Gothic porches of the Ile-de-France and Champagne.

It is in the mature works of Romanesque art and in their Provençal heirs that this exceedingly interesting process of sculptural development and thematic regrouping takes place; it can be traced right up to the birth of early Gothic art. At the beginning all that is representative is concentrated in the tympanum, with an effect of the utmost solemnity, often even a high degree of drama. The archivolt remains as bare as the slightly moulded jambs (Beaulieu, Carennac, Plates 131, 133). Only on the projecting side-walls do we occasionally find narrative and moralizing themes. Later the archivolts and jambs are enriched with more sculptural representations; magnificent, standing statues appear, like so many living supports. And in the last phase of mature Romanesque art—once more Chartres presents an unique example—all parts of the portal, even the capitals of the jambs, are covered with representational figures. But the more this sculpture spreads to all parts of the increasingly large portal the more is the tympanum stripped of its dramatic character, to become again the solemn, hieratic centre of the ritual that is enacted around it. A comparison between Moissac and Chartres—the two peaks of Romanesque portal sculpture in France—shows this shifting emphasis with great clarity.

Already in the first decades of the Gothic style the relationship of the transom to the tympanum, originally constructive, changes into a decorative division of all that is within the archivolt into single registers. It appears already in isolated cases in late Romanesque art; and with it begins the intrinsic decline of the once dominant tympanum.

There can be no doubt that Romanesque art found its truest expression in the carving of supports and capitals; in later styles we encounter façade- and portal-sculpture, while even mural painting—"cette fée qui prodigue le bien ou le mal", as Viollet-le-Duc remarked—is not wholly absent in any century or style. Yet of all the post-antique styles Romanesque art is the only one that gives to the capital not only a constructive and decorative, but also an eminently significant narrative function. The capital, which like a "little head" terminates the pillar at the top and prepares for and supports the semicircular arch, is the real articulation in the Romanesque organism. It is in this connection that we may speak of an *"opus Romanum"*, of an after-effect of classical ideas. For in antique art, which never knew a "Gothic" phase, the semicircle as the basic form of the arch and the vault was never seriously questioned. In one respect only does the Romanesque style show a different, much more abstract conception: it employs the square pillar and the sheaf pillar, which even took the form of an individual monument in the Lantern of the Dead (Plates 180, 199), and very soon also the articulated pillar with a square core decorated with delicate reliefs in semicircles or projecting pier shafts; but it avoids the genuine column with classical entasis. The most usual form of support is the round pillar, which we know in all its variations from the short, heavy type to the tall, slender one. Our illustrations show a great variety of these pillars which even in the same building often show widely differing proportions, since these are nowhere rigidly determined. Above them the capitals burgeon in all their glory. Since in Romanesque art there is no true supporting column without a capital, the number of Romanesque capitals in France is legion. According to Lavedan the church of Saint-Sernin in Toulouse (Plate 101) alone has 600 capitals, and in other buildings there must have been just as many, at Cluny probably even more. Not without cause did Bernard of Clairvaux protest against this splendour of *"coram legentibus fratribus"*.

The size of these capitals ranges from the thin slab of the early structures, in which the capital only marks the boundary between the pillar and the arch (Tournus, Plate 5), through the simply formed chamfered capital or the chip-cut block (Plates 18, 63, 67, 68) to the perfectly carved figure or foliate capital. And as to the thematic representations, there is no limit to the scope of the sculptor's imagination. We find the motif of the interlaced band as a last echo of the carving of the migration period; elements derived from the antique, strictly Ionic capital; the completely stylized foliate capital, from which by a highly interesting process of selection the early Gothic crocketed capital was to emerge; and, above all, the narrative capital, on which—since any religious statement can find a place there—we see the whole gamut of forms. Since our illustrations show an abundance of examples, only two special problems need be mentioned here.

In view of the great number of capitals found in some churches (Vézelay, Plates 33, 34, Autun, Plates 21, 23, 24, Saint-Benoît-sur-Loire, Plates 226–229), where the narrative scene always recurs at the same place in the series of pillars, the spectator may well seek the significance of the iconographical sequence. He will find that the arrangement is arbitrary. Although on occasion there is some kind of group-order, nowhere do we discover a complete programme which might lead the spectator from scene to scene and thus dovetail each one into an organically connected whole. Marie Lefrançois-Pillon speaks bluntly of a "confusion, qui ne serait pas beaucoup plus grande, si l'emplacement en avait été tiré au sort".

The mighty basilica of Saint-Benoît-sur-Loire which owes its name to the fact that it is the resting-place for the body of St Benedict, contains among a very large number of impressive capitals ten which represent the life of the Saint. But they are to be found arbitrarily distributed among all the others, both in the narthex and at the crossing; one is in the nave itself and two high up in the triforium of the choir. Only in later Romanesque art, where the round pillars of the choir-ambulatory surrounding the high altar are included in the plastic decoration, do the capitals of these pillars have a mutual relationship which unites them symbolically with the altar in their midst. Here we must also mention the choir-capitals of the third church of Cluny (Plates 13–15) which contain as a group complete in itself the seven modes of the Gregorian chant.

The impression of unfathomable mystery revealed here is considerably heightened when we turn to the second problem: the great number of monsters and fabulous beings which are nowhere to be found in such abundance as on the Romanesque capitals of France. Henri Focillon calls them: "ce monde inextricable et obscur," and doubtless he meant to indicate that even where a theological explanation can elucidate what these representations are meant to symbolize, the modern beholder still experiences—apart from his admiration for the often enchanting beauty of the carving—a feeling of bewilderment at something unsolved and insoluble. Did not even the erudite contemporary theologian Bernard, Abbott of Clairvaux speak of a "ridicula monstruositas", thereby inaugurating the great process of Gothic disenchantment which in a few decades reduced all this splendour to nothing?

Naturally, a deeper theological and moralizing significance underlies this world of monsters: they represent the innumerable personifications of the evil inherent in mankind, against which the true believer will be warned and even protected by this stark and fantastic display. It is scarcely possible for us today to recognize the far-fetched ancient pagan ideas that have found their ultimate personification here. The numerous references by experts to links with a Celtic past, with forms dating from the migration period, with Oriental themes, with ancient belief in departed spirits and so on, indicate but a few of the problems involved in a larger question which in any case can probably only be partially resolved. Perhaps some of these representations, for instance the "monstres affrontés", were stripped of their former significance already in the Romanesque period and served only as decoration. Yet the great majority of these capitals were doubtless intended to speak with inexorable emphasis to the faithful and to the poor sinner confronted by them.

Whilst plastic ornamentation always remained concentrated at certain points and zones, painting was much more widely distributed over Romanesque churches. If we include stained glass, there is practically no place inaccessible to the painter's brush. Even the capitals and the shafts of the pillars, if they did not bear plastic ornamentation, were frequently and liberally decorated with paint. Furthermore the sculpture itself was generally coloured: the capitals of Civaux (Plates 173, 174) and of Chauvigny (Plates 177–179) serve as special examples of this. The semicircular barrel-vaults of the naves, the flat ceilings or the groined vaults (Saint-Savin, Saint-Chef, Plates 182, 62) allowed the mural paintings to overflow on to the ceilings; the painter used the whole interior as his province. Only in a few chapels such as those of Berzé-la-Ville (Plates 16, 17) and Saint-Chef, or in crypts such as the one at Tavant (Plate 208), can we understand the rôle which mural painting once played: that of transforming the whole space in a spiritual sense and lifting the faithful into the pure world of religious vision, even into the realm of divine grace.

Our plates give numerous examples from all over France and illustrate at the same time the great differences in style between the various districts. The standard works of Henri Focillon, Paul Deschamps and Marc Thibout have made these paintings widely known. This applies especially to the wall and ceiling frescoes of the unique abbey-church of Saint-Savin (Plates 182–186), which are distributed over four different parts of the building, and which led Focillon to honour this church with the title of the "Sistine Chapel" of medieval France. Saint-Savin has long been acknowledged as one of the most important monuments in Europe.

In these Romanesque paintings of France one characteristic of the Romanesque style—the supernatural and the transcendental—is more purely and more magnificently expressed than in any other form of art. There can be no doubt that painting, confined as it is to the surface, most fully realizes the abstract, thereby achieving the fullest expression of transcendentalism and the world beyond. The figure of Christ who replaces God the Father in the scenes of the Creation in Saint-Savin (Plate 185) is of such sublime majesty that the contemporary works of sculpture are overshadowed by it. It seems as if this figure of Christ was meant to illustrate that famous dictum of Anselm of Canterbury: "All that exists, exists only thanks to a single cause, and this cause which is the only power that exists through itself—is God." This was written during exactly the same period, at the end of the eleventh century. The host of angels on the walls and on the vaults of the upper chapel of the transept at Saint-Chef (Plate 62) are of such immaterial transparency and unearthly remoteness that they seem to have just floated down from on high to surround and serve the Redeemer enthroned in the crown of the vault. No wonder that in the same decades stained glass—the very nature of which represents a further step towards unreality and transparency—was able to celebrate its first great triumphs.

But this brings us to the cardinal question with which all art-historical research is concerned: the question of the relationship between the style and what it strove to express. To what inner compulsion does this world of visions owe its origin?

III

Those holding the usual ideas as to the course of the history of European styles, who quietly peruse the plates in this book, will be surprised at the variety of the modes of expression here represented. And we hope for readers who, recollecting vivid artistic impressions, will examine both the text and the pictures thoughtfully and critically. In contrast to the figure of Christ in the "Temptation" at Plaimpied (Plate 165), which together with the mural paintings at Vicq (Plates 162, 163) comes closest to the "Baroque" pole of Romanesque art, we have the totally different Christ of the "Temptation" at Saulieu, which, with its delicate lyrical quality, is a typical example of fine Burgundian Romanesque art. Again, the figures on the capitals at Besse-en-Chandesse (Plate 152) representing the "Death of the Rich Man" seem to be modelled on some relief of the migration period, while the "Women at the Holy Sepulchre" on a capital of Mozac (Plate 153) are conceived with an almost classical serenity. And the artistic contrast between the two representations of "Daniel in the Lions' Den" in Charlieu (Plates 58, 59) is so great that one might be tempted to regard the bas-relief as a fragment incorporated from a more ancient building.

The same applies to architecture whose manifold types we have already mentioned. Our illustrations begin and end with an early Romanesque monastic church of the eleventh century: Tournus (Saint-Philibert) and Ottmarsheim (Plates 1, 271). Yet the difference in the spatial structure of these two churches could not be greater. For, simultaneously with the heavy pillared basilica at Tournus, an octagonal domed church with a two-storeyed octagonal ambulatory was erected on the Upper Rhine, which in its turn recalls the five-domed "Byzantine" church at Périgueux (Plates 187, 188), as well as the Rotunda of Charroux (Plate 175)—based on an early Christian conception.

What we have stated here about the structural type of the buildings as a whole is also valid for the interior organization of the parts: the arrangement of the nave and the chapels, the choice of supports and the vaulting. The variety of ways in which the architectural problems have been solved and the passion for finding new solutions is surprising. It even extends to those cases where something like a norm had been evolved in the mother-church of an Order. Scarcely had the plan of the second church of Cluny—a pillared basilica with a nave and two aisles, circular barrel vaults over the nave and groined cross-vaults over the aisles and an *échelon* choir—been determined at the end of the tenth century, at least for the new foundations of the Order—and even there with some difficulty—than Cluny itself changed its system and adapted it to the great pilgrims' churches. And this new, gigantic third building at Cluny, begun in 1089, with two transepts and an ambulatory with radiating chapels—whose most faithful surviving copy is at Paray-le-Monial (Plates 44-46)—was scarcely finished, when at Clairvaux, an abbey of the same Burgundian district, the counter-movement set in, leading in its turn to a completely new organization of the interior arrangement in the first churches of the Cistercian Order.

In Romanesque architecture there is no comprehensive system of building that meets every requirement, as represented by the Gothic cathedral that was to evolve at the end of the twelfth century. There is no unifying principle in the content of Romanesque sculpture, such as the Gothic style was subsequently to show as a result of the study of nature. Briefly, the Romanesque style as a whole—unlike all later styles—has no over-all norm for controlling the inner and outer form. For the only overriding and all-embracing moulding force of Romanesque art is the conception of God, as the creator of the world, as a power not of the material but of the spiritual world. It is this that grants the artist such immense freedom.

This freedom, this lack of a compulsory material norm, explains another artistic peculiarity of the Romanesque style, that both stimulates scientific surmise and fascinates the eye of modern man; namely, the capacity to absorb and use older, strange, and even apparently heterogeneous forms. While it is a generally accepted law that in sculptural style single elements from former periods live on as part of the decoration or as simple ornaments, we believe that in Romanesque art we can recognize a whole series of legacies from more ancient styles. We find portrayals of figures in Celtic style; others, conceived in the spirit of ancient Rome, on arcades and capitals. The great migrations seem to live on in numerous carvings and ornaments; buildings are modelled on Byzantine architecture; while contemporary styles come in with Catalan frescoes from the south and Lombard portals from the east. As in Scandinavian Romanesque the runic language still lives on, so French Romanesque art is pervaded by forms from all the older cultures with which the inhabitants of France had been in contact, both inside and outside its frontiers. Romanesque art became the great repository for all these forms.

Later they were to be fused with the real, organic elements of the style, to constitute more and more of a unity. The absence of a norm is also everywhere apparent in the details, in the whole or parts of the buildings, in a single scene or figure, in a single limb or gesture. Everywhere, even in the fiercest battle scenes, the sculpture declares its spiritual autonomy, is isolated and remote. Even superficially this is already apparent in the fluctuating size of the figures, for which the Burgundian tympana of Vézelay and Autun (Plates 33, 20) may serve as examples; it is manifest in the monumental, often masklike and stereotyped moulding of the faces, even where figures are combined in an animated group; and it is manifest above all where single figures stand side by side enshrined in an arcade. The charming little façade of AzayleRideau (Plate 210) exemplifies this specifically Romanesque peculiarity.

But the desire for isolation and autonomy becomes especially apparent in the situation of a number of churches. No other churches stand so high and so completely isolated as do the Romanesque ones. Later, during the Gothic period, when churches were built in the centre of urban areas, they were daringly constructed in an attempt to raise them as far as possible above the human zone, but this must be considered as something of a travesty of the truly heroic efforts of Romanesque art to situate the House of God as near to God as possible. The church on the Mont SaintMichel, once the crowning pinnacle of a steep, isolated rock in the ocean (Plate 247), and the Chapel of SaintMicheld'Aiguilhe at Le Puy (Plate 137), testify just as clearly to this tendency as does, say, the Monastery of SaintGuilhemleDésert (Plate 98) which, magnificently situated in utter isolation, is expressive even in name of the longing to turn away from all worldly things.

We must look for a deeper explanation for all these peculiarities of the Romanesque style. It must naturally take into account all such influences, associations, migrations of motifs and so forth as critical research has established; but at bottom it can only proceed from the moment when the creative artist is confronted by his subject, whether freely chosen or imposed upon him. Then we find the effective, creative synthesis between the two fundamental components: the artist's impulse to create on the one hand and the thing to be produced on the other. It is an old truth that in this synthesis the artist strives to give material expression to his innermost feelings, and this fact is no less valid for Romanesque art than for any of the later or earlier styles.

The uniqueness of the Romanesque style lies in the special character of the subject with which the artist was confronted and so of the creative process that produced the work of art. Viewed superficially, this subject-matter seems to be essentially of our world. There are human beings, animals, plants, sun and moon and everything else pertaining to the earthly theme. But none of these are there for their own sake. They are there to represent and express the cause of all life, namely, God, as Anselm of Canterbury stressed. Nevertheless this "subject" of art, the power of God, is so comprehensive and mighty that, when the artist meets it, it penetrates to the innermost fibres of his artistic imagination, and so everything he creates bears the stamp of its spirit. The Romanesque work of art has but one meaning and is completely dominated by God.

That is why in Romanesque art the personality of the artist remains veiled, whereas it will impetuously demand its rights in Gothic art. Were it to manifest itself more distinctly in Romanesque art, the omnipotence of God would be impaired. For where a general principle is all-powerful, the individual must be silent and withdraw. And since the individuality of the creative artist recedes, there can be no individual forms in the work he creates. Nor does the individuality of the spectator play a decisive rôle, and the carvings and paintings, regardless of whether they can be seen or not, make no rational concessions to the faithful. The "threefold reflection of the personality", one of the fundamental laws of all art, is here revealed in its primary stage as a threefold expression of the impersonal.

Viewed in this light the many peculiarities of Romanesque style become fully compre-hensible: the solitude and isolation of buildings and people—how could they come nearer to God than on the topmost summit of a rock or "in eremo"? The absence of a norm—how should any norm at all exist in the face of the omnipotence of God? For such a norm could only derive from human beings, as it did later in Gothic art. Like any obtrusion of the personality of the artist it would mean a belittling of God, an intrusion into His presence. Seen in perspective, Roman-esque art undoubtedly steers a middle course between the Mosaic-Byzantine ban on images on the one hand, and the anthropomorphism of later times on the other. For the old iconoclasts the mere idea of representing the Deity in human form seemed like severing some earthly part from the divine essence as a whole; in Romanesque art the great authority of men like Anselm of Canterbury was needed to moderate this conception, for "He who forgives sins, belongs to the same race as the sinner himself." In the scenes of the Creation in Saint-Savin (Plate 185) we already saw the path for which Romanesque art was searching: these scenes represent God as a human being, but in the loftiest aspect of human power yet known—in Christ. That is why Christ, serving—as it were—a double function, is the most solemn and sublime figure of Romanesque art. As judge of the world he is enthroned in solemn majesty in the tympanum and moves like an unapproachable magician through the splendour of the capitals and the mural paintings.

We open up a last chapter of this fascinating process when we recall the dominating rôle of the symbol. Without doubt Romanesque art, in its language of symbols—figurative as well as non-figurative—has created one of its most magnificent modes of expression. No other style in European art has made such a powerful use of symbolism, and nowhere is Romanesque symbolism so powerful as in France. In the light of the process we have just described this passion for symbolism which breaks out everywhere can be readily understood. It teaches us that everything that exists in the world represents nothing less than an image of the divine power; consequently it is a symbol of the presence of God and His rule. Indeed, the universe itself forms in its entirety a single grand majestic symbol.

Thus it can happen that the powers of darkness, the passions of the sinner's soul, become incarnate in fabulous beings and monsters which—influenced perhaps by late antique conceptions—no longer have any recognizable shape, but are purely hybrid creatures. Moreover, the human figure where it appears can be depicted in a variety of forms, now assuming the organic beauty of a classical statue, now reduced to a graphic sign; now only a fraction of the man is portrayed, now he actually merges with entirely alien elements, and thus ceases to be human. But man only renounces his hereditary shape because—like everything in Romanesque art—he serves a higher Power and by symbolically proclaiming the greatness of this Power, he becomes himself again in a higher sense. Such is the world of Romanesque ideas in its purest form.

MARCEL POBÉ

A PILGRIMAGE THROUGH ROMANESQUE FRANCE

ROMANESQUE ART IN FRANCE—French Romanesque Art—Romanesque France—archaeologists and art historians have accustomed us to such titles and definitions. When they discuss the art of the eleventh and twelfth centuries, they immediately think of the geographical area of present-day France and use it as a fixed framework for their theme. We shall do the same here: our illustrations depict nothing which is outside modern France, while the France envisaged by our text has the physical boundaries determined by the Second World War. But this current method of classifying and defining the art of bygone ages according to the geography of our own time requires a word of explanation.

We say "France"—and visualize a country bounded by three seas: the Mediterranean, the Atlantic Ocean, the Channel as a link with the North Sea—and by three mountain ranges: the Jura, the Alps, the Pyrenees, with, in the north-east, the dangerously unguarded gap on the left bank of the Rhine. It must, however, be understood that these familiar frontiers take on the nature of an arbitrary choice when we begin to deal with the geographical expansion of an art for whose origin we have to look back eight or nine centuries. For, in this context they embrace a variety of districts—mostly independent and differing widely from one another—which together represent a still emergent France, and even that only partially.

It is precisely this manifold character, which on the one hand is ignorant of national centralization and on the other feels the impact of the birth of political nationalism, that is so strongly expressed in Romanesque art. As has already been indicated, Romanesque art is young and new and infinitely varied. Recent events—wars and revolutions that have caused profound political changes, destroyed and created states and entailed vast movements of populations, such as the West had not experienced for a long time—have taught us again how relative frontiers are. He who is unable to grasp this sense of geographical relativity erects barriers for himself, blinds himself from the very outset to the historical understanding of Romanesque art as here discussed. The present frontiers of France are both too wide and too narrow when it comes to encompassing that intellectual world which—for the sake of an easy definition—we venture to call French Romanesque art.

This sounds paradoxical and calls at once for a further explanation. Too wide? That is understandable. But too narrow? If we wish to define the actual spread of Romanesque art which is "French" in spirit and "French" in origin, its frontiers would reach in the west, say, to Santiago di Compostella and in the east to Syria and Palestine. Both early and, more especially, recent Spanish research has revealed with increasing clarity what architectural consistency of style, and how many related sculptural motifs—showing how fertile has been the migration of cultural ideas—are to be found along the pilgrims' route to Santiago. We have already mentioned how, in the enlargement of a given type of building for a specific purpose, the so-called pilgrims' churches may be compared with similar churches within France and beyond its frontiers, above all with the Cathedral of St James the Greater at the end of the "French route", as the Spaniards themselves call that stretch of the pilgrims' way which passes through their territory.

In the coastal district of Asia Minor, occupied by the Franks for two centuries after the first crusade, certain sculptures seem to derive from the same imaginative concepts—may even be the work of the same artists—as the surprisingly similar carvings in Berry, south of the great curve of the Loire. Such a sculpture, for instance, as the "Devil" in the Temptation at Plaimpied (Plate 164) is to be found in the same thin and hairy form digging his claws into a capital at Nazareth. (Paul Deschamps actually placed plaster-casts of such carvings side by side with the reproductions of French sculpture in the strict national sense, in the Musée des Monuments Français in Paris.) So, too, Norman Romanesque art—a branch of "French" Romanesque art— spreads still further afield, though it represents the art of the most ruthless foreign invaders' immediate descendants. From northern France it spread over a great part of England, culminating indeed in such churches and cathedrals as Durham, Norwich, Winchester, Peterborough, the Romanesque portions of which clearly show their origin. Yes, this distinctive style even migrated with the Normans to Sicily. A last example, nearer to the present frontiers, but still beyond them, is the baptismal font of St Ulrich in the Black Forest. This really monumental work of art, with a diameter of over two and a half metres, bears a distinctly early-Burgundian character in its sculptural ornament which, beginning with a figure of Christ with the four symbols of the Evangelists, runs on either side right round the font; the stone from which the figures of the apostles and prophets are carved comes from Burgundy, as geologists have been able to prove. It was probably a present from the mother-church of Cluny to the priory in the Breisgau which had joined the great monastic reform movement; for the Benedictine monks of Cluny—as later did the Cistercian monks of Citeaux and especially of Clairvaux—spread their movement over the whole Christian West. Thus a masterpiece of Burgundian art was able to carry "French" inspiration beyond the Rhine. We could easily add to the number of such examples. They prove that French Romanesque art is, to say the least, too narrowly confined by the present frontiers of France. And yet in other instances these same frontiers are too wide. We need only think of Alsace, which indubitably belongs to France today. Its Romanesque art—as exemplified in the high, flat chancel-wall behind the huge twin-towered transept of Murbach (Plate 266), the west façades of Marmoutier and Sélestat (Plate 262), the sculptures in the elaborate narthex of Lautenbach (Plates 267–270) which seem to be very archaic considering their date, and even the domed octagonal church of Ottmarsheim on the upper Rhine (Plate 271) which recalls Carolingian art—is obviously more closely related to Rhineland art than to the schools of central France, even though Burgundian influence crossed the Vosges. In the Roussillon, in the extreme south-west of France, we find buildings which display, together with Mozarabic features, peculiarities which are characteristic of Catalonian Romanesque art, as found beyond the Pyrenees. Such are the horse-shoe arch and the geometrical ornaments in Saint-Michel-de-Cuxa, or the famous wall-paintings of Saint-Martin-de-Fenouillar (Plate 109), of which Marc Thibout rightly says: "The paintings on the French side of the Pyrenees belong to the Catalonian school, which displays qualities very unlike those of the other Romanesque paintings preserved in France." And yet at the time of their origin Catalonia had come under French sovereignty. If we move up the Rhône Valley towards the Alps, we find in Provence—which was only incorporated into France in 1486—not only some of the above-mentioned porticoes with slim outer columns supported on the backs of couching lions, as at Digne and Embrun (Plate 83), but also typical Lombard towers (Plate 84), some of which actually stand at a little distance from the church. The towers of the priory of Saint-Symphorien, south of Apt, are a typical example, and give one the impression of being in Italy.

Under the first king of the Capetian dynasty, that is, during the Romanesque period, the recognized frontiers of France were still frequently changing. The first Romanesque architecture —such as, for instance, the "westwork" of Tournus (Plates 2, 4–7) with which our illustrations begin—more or less coincides in date with the foundation of the new, the first really French, dynasty. Hugh, surnamed Capet, was elected King of the Franks in 987. His son, Robert II, called the Pious, was king in the year 1000. During the period of less than two centuries which covers the reigns of Henry I (crowned in 1031), Philip I (1060), Louis VI (1108), Louis VII (1137) and Philip II (1180–1223), the once "royal domain" confined to an area between the Seine and the Loire, expanded continuously and became the real Frankish kingdom. By the time Gothic art was created it was already in control of a considerably enlarged and fortified territory with adequate safeguards against rebellious vassals. Most of the Romanesque works which we show here originated outside the "royal domain", but increasingly the sovereignty of the king extended over the territories in which they were created.

If we wish to understand the political and spiritual situation which led to the rise of Romanesque art, it is necessary to cast a quick glance at the preceding development, since it teaches us to appreciate that cultural renaissance of which Romanesque art remains the most visible testimony.

Gaul, which was once overpowered by the Roman legions but later revitalized by Latin civilization and awakened spiritually by the spread of Christianity, did not simply disappear at the fall of the Roman empire. For half a millennium it was subject to continual change imposed first by the storm and stress, then by the gradual cessation of the great migrations. Despite the continual flow through its lands of Teutonic tribes, who gradually colonized them, France remained faithful to the Roman language, adopted from its former conquerors—the Langue d'oc in the south, and in the north the Langue d'oïl with its more marked vowel changes—though, admittedly, numerous Germanic forms were added to the Celtic and Roman names. So the population of the country preserved in the depths of an enduring subconscious nationalism its originally Gallic character—the obstinate individualism, the alert love of everything new and alien as well as the sense of order and the craving for civilization instilled by the Romans. The *civitates* and the *pagi* continued to form the basis of French civilization, but fresh Teutonic trends were superimposed upon Celtic elements and the Roman tradition. Hence the new rural colonization, which for a long time retained a certain mobility, preferring the country to settlement in towns. Coarse manners replaced refined living. Art, which had exhausted itself in the late Gallo-Roman period, gained certain new impulses, but where it emancipated itself from copying antique forms, it did not rise above the level of craftsmanship.

Throughout this transformation Gaul remained faithful to a single sustaining power that outlasted everything: the Christian faith, which was able to act as a leaven even in a world that seemed to have changed its way of life. After the arrival of the still partly pagan "barbarians", Christendom simply took up anew its universal missionary work on the soil of Gaul. Success was not slow in coming: the baptism of Clovis in the last year of the fifth century represents a turning-point. And since the danger of Arianism—which heresy had long continued to attract a number of immigrants—was also finally overcome, there existed at least one factor for binding together the new conglomeration of peoples now occupying the ancient land of Gaul: unity in the Christian faith. Thus centuries of autochthonous religious faith form the background of Romanesque art; it could build upon the Credo which had become the essence of a Gaul transformed.

But political unity of the region which we are discussing here was still in the future, to be realized only when Gaul became France. Strangely enough, even the transformed Gaul remains faithful to the old, never abandoned idea of Empire. The Empire remains a potential unifying power; as an idea, it extends far beyond Gaul, and for a short time takes visible shape under Charlemagne—the one sovereign that France and Germany have had in common. To sum up, we may echo the words of the historian Gonzague de Reynold: "Avant l'idée de France, il y eut celle de la mission impériale et chrétienne."

Certainly this double mission achieved notable success in the ninth century. But it was not a lasting one. When considering our western spiritual heritage, we must never forget the Carolingian contribution. Much that the new emperor of the West had called into being and had first flourished during his reign, was revived and found full expression in Romanesque art; for example, the wall- and ceiling-paintings in Auxerre, Ternand and a few other places, achievements from before 1000, were to have a decisive influence on the later style. Numerous Romanesque buildings arose on the foundations of former Carolingian structures. At Charlieu we find the remains of a Romanesque church built on the ruins of a Carolingian basilica, from which comes the relief of "Daniel in the Lions' Den" (Plate 59). Beside the impressive ruins of Notre-Dame at Jumièges (Plate 256) still stand the more modest, but no less venerable walls of the first bays of a Carolingian church dedicated to St Peter. Often Romanesque builders continued to work on Carolingian structures which in those turbulent times had never been completed, or on sites where the already finished Carolingian edifice had been destroyed.

For the century immediately preceding the Romanesque era presents a gloomy picture. Political decay is accompanied by cultural decline, and to the internal disintegration are added terrible invasions from outside, which recall the times of the Huns. It seems that the forces which served to maintain political unity and defence, as well as to consolidate Occidental civilization, instead of being linked together, slackened again and became disrupted. Conditions in Gaul at that time were worse than the earlier chaotic ones under the Merovingians—for now it was a case of reversion to anarchy. The hydra-headed feudal system—"cette plaie mortelle de l'Etat", as Daniel-Rops bitterly but accurately defines it—began to split up the young empire, though admittedly it created social ties which bound men together into a community by an oath of fidelity. These bonds pertained to a man, the feudal lord, not to a country, let alone a state; they implied dependence from above and from below without the stratified relationship of an organized society. Such bonds involved men in the petty egotism of feuding neighbours, and in rivalries that influenced Romanesque building activity, sometimes hampering, sometimes stimulating it. But since a central authority which could lay down the law and arbitrate was lacking, the individual as vassal remained at the mercy of the feudal lord.

For the most part this was a bad thing, since the decline of the Carolingian Empire brought not only neglect but disaster. Famines broke out where farming was neglected. Epidemics decimated the population who lived among ruins. There was no arable land for the fugitives retreating before the invaders, for the cleared forest areas were soon abandoned. The general state of insecurity meant that even commerce could scarcely maintain its established organizations and its centuries-old trade-routes. In the early Romanesque period all these troubles existed as a threatening reality; later they continued as evil memories, oppressing the contemporary imagination like a nightmare.

The invasions which devastated the West, and which modern man can again visualize only too vividly with his mind's eye, played an especially important rôle until the eleventh century. Following one another, or even overlapping, they kept the West, on three sides, in a state of almost uninterrupted fear and anxiety. France, in particular, was exposed to the invasions of pirates. From the middle of the ninth century onwards, the Normans had been crossing the North Sea and the Atlantic Ocean, a last Scandinavian wave, as it were, of the Germanic migrations. They were skilful navigators who in their easily handled boats—the "Drakkars"—could even row up the rivers. Individual groups of them settled down at the beginning of the tenth century at the mouth of the Seine and, later, of the Loire; others went pillaging from place to place, while overland from the east a new menace appeared: hordes of Hungarians. Like the Huns in former times, these Magyars—also Asiatic—advanced, burning and ravaging as far as the Loire, and down the Rhône valley as far as Arles; from the Mediterranean, the Saracens remained a constant threat. The Islamic empire had encircled the Christian West. The horsemen of Allah had their fortified strongholds not only in North Africa, not only over wide tracts of the Iberian peninsula, but also in Sicily and South Italy, even on the coast of Provence. From the range of mountains, the Maures—said to be named after them—these Moors carried their raids far northward, into Savoy, where we find the analogously named Maurienne. And there was no Charles Martel to confront them with unified resistance.

At the close of the first millennium of the Christian era all these invaders, whether pagan Teutons or Asians, or Mohammedan Arabs, struck terror into the hearts of the inhabitants of the western countries, thus substantially influencing the world scene at that time. If to this we add internal wars and highway robbery, it is not surprising that—quite apart from the part played by fear of the year 1000—these people, continually beset by peril, lived their lives in the shadow of the most sombre prophecies and apocalyptic visions. It is only natural that this attitude to life should find expression also in the art of the period. Its influence can readily be detected in the history of the origin of many settlements and buildings.

The former abbey-church of Tournus, which we purposely put at the beginning of our pictorial section—for it is paradigmatic in more than one respect—serves as a clear example. In 836 the monks of Noirmoutier left their island on the Atlantic coast which was particularly exposed to the Norman marauders. As their greatest treasure they took with them the mortal remains of St Philibert who, in the seventh century, had established their rule under the influence of the Benedictine Order and St Columban's spirit of reform. Several times their flight was checked, but in the end it led them through the whole of Gaul from west to east: Anjou—Poitou—Auvergne—Burgundy. Finally in 875 they settled on the right bank of the

Saône in the former abbey of St Valérien. The new settlement was responsible for a change of name: the monastery became Saint-Philibert de Tournus. Only sixty years later the newly occupied monastery was pillaged and destroyed by Hungarians invading from the east and had to be rebuilt. A further calamity must also be mentioned: in 1006 the abbey was severely damaged by fire. Thus the building as we see it—more or less intact—today, was erected on successive ruins.

Elsewhere the influence of the invasions made itself felt in the situation and the particular construction of the churches and monasteries. Numerous Romanesque buildings of the Rhône valley and the country east of it stand like castles on high hills; along the river valley this may have been due to the fear of its periodical inundations, as at Vion (Plate 64) or at La Garde-Adhémar (Plate 69); but in the almost waterless Haute-Provence, the church had to offer protection only against invasions (Plate 78). The church of the Saintes-Maries-de-la-Mer at the south border of the Camargue, provided at the outset with high walls, was subsequently completed as a real fortress (Plate 97). It is also understandable that on the insecure and much-contested frontier of the Pyrenees entire monasteries should take on the characteristics of a fortress, as for instance Saint-Martin-du-Canigou and Saint-Michel-de-Cuxa (Plates 112, 113).

The iconography of the porches and capitals, too, is informative. Some sculptures tell of terrifying enemies who were bent on pillaging the treasures of the Church. One of the most interesting pieces of evidence is offered by a detail in the marble sculptures of the porch of Oloron-Sainte-Marie, where fettered Saracens are made, like Atlantids, to bear the load of the tympanum (Plate 119). On the tympanum itself the Descent from the Cross is depicted, and below it we see two groups of lions—the one on the left representing the persecuted Church, and the one on the right the liberated Church (Plate 117). In the abbey-church of Saint-Martin-de-Boscherville, dedicated to the sainted knight and dragon-killer George, massive capitals above the huge cylinder-like columns which carry the so-called "Norman" gallery show, next to savage hunting-scenes, a number of pagan emblems of typical Teutonic design. Notwithstanding the fact that those responsible for the building were baptized, these emblems have managed to find their way into the sanctuary—that is, into the arms of the transept—and so, suffered or possibly even welcomed by the Church, they represent the homage and submission of the converted Normans to their new God.

SPIRIT

More forcibly than in such outward manifestations the rigours of those days live on in the general mood which today still—or rather, today in particular—grips us with elemental force at the sight of Romanesque art; above all, its sculpture, which breathes the spirit of the age. The numerous battle scenes can only be the result of an immediately experienced reality, although they often have a symbolic, metaphorical significance pertaining to the moral and spiritual life. Also attributable to the atrocities of those times is the repeated impression of horror and the uncanny, by which the beholder is often more deeply affected than by the artistic beauty of the work. The Flight into Egypt (Plate 23) or the Massacre of the Innocents—from which the child Jesus escapes—need no literary model to be depicted correctly. The tortures of the martyrs—be it the roasting of St Lawrence (Plate 16) or the stoning of St Stephen (Plate 90), even the individual stages of the Passion of Christ (Plate 163), are not represented theoretically, but have their origin in some appalling concrete experience which the artist had seen with his own eyes.

Needless to say, the Church with its pedagogical morality traces all disaster—invasions, wars, famines, epidemics—back to the misdeeds of the faithful who have not lived according to Christian doctrine. And indeed, as always in times of confusion, hand in hand with material decline goes a general corruption of morals about which the surviving chronicles of this and the following period tell us bluntly enough. For the theologian, as for the art inspired by his teaching, such sinfulness incurs due retribution—and history often serves to support this view. The Hungarians are a new "scourge of God", all types of marauding a just punishment for bad Christians. Fear of the consequences of sin makes sin itself—above all, the wickedness of the deadly sins—appear as the terrible origin of all evil. The original sin of the first humans, with Eve's temptation by the devil-serpent (Plate 22) and the expulsion from Paradise are among the most frequently and variously represented subjects of the Old Testament. The first murder, too, is often depicted: the murder of his innocent brother Abel by Cain, together with the preceding story of Abel's sacrifice which pleased God, and Cain's which God rejected. The illustration of the deadly sin of Avaritia (Plate 125), dramatically bitten by toads and serpents, shows that the death of the miser (Plate 152), who ignored the starving multitudes, is fearful. That of Luxuria no less clearly shows that harlotry and fornication, which lead to terrible consequences, must be severely punished.

The horror which sin and the punishment of sin produces is set forth nowhere more impressively than in the various representations of the Devil, the personification of evil, the founder of all harm, whom not even Emile Mâle can trace back to some Oriental prototype but has to recognize as a pure invention of the Romanesque sculptors' terrified imagination. "Ce n'est pas à l'imagination orientale que le moyen âge doit ce terrible Satan des chapiteaux du XIIème siècle." No, the "Mile Artifex", the conjurer, as he is called on a capital at Brioude, was observed at his work everywhere in the eleventh century. When the vicious man dies, Satan tears his soul out of his mouth (Plate 152); in the opposite case, the soul of the Saint is received and carried to Heaven by angels. As the opponent of the Heavenly Judge of the world, Satan, on the Day of Judgment, carries the condemned to Hell (Plates 20, 135). He is even allowed to tempt the Son of God Himself, become man, as St Matthew and St Luke each testify in the Scriptures.

On a well-known capital in Saulieu the Burgundian sculptor represents Christ with an angel standing behind Him. Christ himself stands in quiet, compelling majesty, holding the open Book in His left hand, while His right hand is raised to emphasize his teaching. "It is written: Man does not live by bread alone, but by every word that goeth forth from the mouth of God." As opposed to this, a sculptor of Berry, on the other side of the Loire, vividly depicts on a capital at Plaimpied (Plates 164, 165) the third, purely spiritual temptation of Christ. We really feel the full horror of the monstrous demand to adore the spirit of evil, who appears in twofold guise dancing before Christ—hairy to the left and serpent-like to the right of Him. The expression on the face and the gesture of the outstretched arms interpret the rebuke: "Get thee behind me, Satan!", which by some devilish transformation, seems even to be repeated realistically in the dragon-shape of the chair. (Plate 27 enables us to compare representations of the Devil.)

The Church at that time used this imperious command: "Get thee behind me, Satan!" as an exorcism, sometimes even as a cry of warning to its followers. With the figure of Satan, partly modelled on the recorded visions of monks, and partly on the still surviving ideas of demons derived from ancient folk-lore—the latter may well have influenced the former—we touch the lowest depths of depravity. From here the road to salvation can only lead upward. After the decline of the pre-Romanesque and early Romanesque century the revival comes with the full maturity of Romanesque art.

If in the history of the Western world it is permissible to use the word "miracle" of any place and at any time, it would be justified here. The sudden change that can be observed from the tenth to the eleventh and twelfth centuries, the cultural reconstruction after the decline, the slow, but persistent rise of a new monarchic dynasty, the conversion of the feudal system into an instrument of order, the moral improvement, especially the reform of the clergy—this is a process as striking and gratifying as it is unexpected. For, after all, the formation and consolidation of Western civilization is part of the process which has moulded our own un-finished history.

Eugène Jarry, geographer and historian, one of the latest authors to trace the growth of French unity, describes the state of Western "Francia", where a central power was lacking, as: "l'état de pulvérisation du pouvoir public à la fin du Xème siècle." From this state of pulveri-zation France gradually emerged, taking shape under the guidance of the Capetian dynasty that had succeeded the last of the Carolingians. The new dynasty, originating in the centre of the region once colonized by the "Romanized" Franks, succeeded in achieving an organic political unity within the steadily growing area of "France". This was a result that neither the Goths who once founded a kingdom between the Pyrenees and the Alps, nor the Burgundians who on several occasions held the Rhine-Rhône line, had achieved, while Charlemagne with his extensive empire did not even attempt it. For a short time, it is true, something more valuable had been achieved: the unification of the West under the Carolingian dynasty. It remains a lasting disaster for Europe that this structure, with its splendid foundations, should have been allowed to fall to pieces again under their successors.

The dynasty of the Capets knew the value of limitation. Looking back in the light of our subsequent knowledge, we must not, of course, endow them with the perspicacity to appreciate that it was desirable to seek political unification within a small framework the moment the Carolingian dispute over the right of succession had again split the state once so happily united. Nevertheless, a significant difference between the political development in the East and in the West is noticeable. As always in the Italo-German area, under the Saxon emperors and continuing under the later dynasties, the grand dream of empire remained, and the attempts to realize it have something heroically tragic about them. In France, however, a new ideal was being pursued: with a kingdom that consciously limited itself, whilst it made no universal claims, was no longer subordinate to an imperial power, the way was prepared for the possible formation of a future nation. Nor did it indulge in adventurous and fateful enterprises, as did the Norman dynasty—which, by the way, came from the same French area—in imposing its rule on what was to become the world-wide empire of the British. That is why the dynasty of the Capets has been accused of lacking vision—a grand, over-all ideal. They had a practical sense of what was attainable *hic et nunc*, they had great patience and shrewd restraint, which enabled them to unite again, piece by piece, with never-flagging perseverance, the *disjecta membra* of one-time Gaul. Certainly there is no dramatic tension in this policy of carefully preserved property, continually enlarged, which the typical French expression "terre à terre" so aptly describes—but it does possess elements of far-reaching logic. Taking a wider view, we must admit that this apparent lack of a sense of adventure, this keen instinct for danger was here simply diverted to a different channel. Why should this love of adventure—heightened by the upheavals of the migrations—not have been carried over from ancient Gaul to modern France? By his very nature the Frenchman prefers to stake his all, over and over again, not for mere material aims, not for political fulfilment, but for the far more enthralling adventure of the spirit.

This gives us the key to the sudden and beautiful flowering of Romanesque art after the year 1000. At that time adventure of the spirit meant exclusively religious adventure. God was implied in the adventure: "*Gesta dei per Francos.*" The first two crusades, which (in the Romanesque period) called the West to arms against Islam, started in France. The real originator of the first crusade, planned at the Council of Clermont in the Auvergne at the end of November 1095, was Pope Urban II, formerly the monk Eudes de Châtillon of the Abbey of Cluny. Peter the Hermit, from Amiens, who was believed to have been delegated by God, summoned the Christian world to join it. Obeying this call, the Christians regained the Holy Sepulchre on July 15th, 1099. And the news of the liberation of Jerusalem that stirred the Western world inspired a Burgundian youth named Bernard, son of Tescelin, a nobleman, and a liegeman of the Duke. Scarcely half a century later this servant of God, who had meanwhile become the famous Abbot of Clairvaux, launched for a second time the hosts of princes and knights on a crusade from Vézelay: "Behold, time is favourable for you now. The days of the abounding mercy have come. The earth trembles, because God in Heaven is losing his earth. I say: this is the earth on which the Word of God was seen and heard and once lived for over thirty years—as a man among men. But now, on account of our sins, the enemies of the Cross have raised their heads. They lay waste the Promised Land with the sword. As your own land abounds in courageous men, it is seemly that you should be the very first to join the forces of the Living God. Forward! Forward! Noble warriors! Gird on your swords! Forsake not your king, the King of the Franks. What do I say? Forsake not the King of Heaven, for whose sake your king undertakes this dangerous expedition." Every word in this appeal reveals the spirit of Romanesque France. Realistic political considerations were not only secretly involved in this bold, idealistic enterprise, but even clearly admitted by Urban II, as when he said that the growing power of the vassals had to be diverted, and the surplus population employed.

But the motto is: *Deus lo volt*—God wishes it. This cry sounded louder than the arguments of careful reasoning. Parallel with the crusades in the south-east is the less spectacular, but no less important *Reconquista* in the south-west. The Spanish peninsula, at the western extremity of which the tomb of St James the Greater attracts hundreds of thousands of pilgrims, must be reconquered for the Christians. In this endless, recurrent movement which Charlemagne, at the end of his life, seems to have divined—since he built an advanced ring of forts from the Mediterranean to the Atlantic on the south side of the Pyrenees—French knights again play the main rôle, not only those from nearby Aquitaine who are immediately interested, but increasing numbers also from beyond the Loire. In the course of some two hundred years—approximately from the middle of the eleventh century to the death in 1252 of Ferdinand III (who was subsequently canonized)—together with the northern Spaniards, they drove Islam out of all its strongholds in the peninsula, with the exception of a small area around Granada. The army of the French knights set out on this crusade from a comparatively narrow strip of territory: Catalonia —Aragon—Navarre—Castile—Asturias—Galicia. Here again many men at a loose end found diverting occupation in a foreign country, while knowing that their deeds pleased God. A further peculiar blend of prudence and temerity gradually put an end to the Norman threat, in this case not by expulsion, but by well-considered assimilation: land for settlement in what was later to become Normandy was given to the newcomers, and missionary monks were sent to convert them; these from the outset defied the hostility roused by their teaching, becoming engaged later in active building. (At almost the same time at the other end of the western world the Hungarians were converted and from a roving menace were made to become a stable element and a permanent barrier against Asia.)

Thus, at the time which we are here discussing, the West was again advancing on several fronts, breaking down frontiers and spreading the doctrine of salvation according to the spirit of the Gospel, in the way Christ himself demanded, which is illustrated on the tympanum above the centre portal at Vézelay (Plate 33). The contribution from France, a country still in the making, was of special importance in that it gave to the movement its initial impetus. Through the crusades in the East the French made repeated contact with the world of the Near East, while the *Reconquista* in the West established a contact of long duration with the ancient civilization of Islam in Spain and with such remaining Christians as were tolerated there, who preserved their faith, but were influenced in many ways by Arab civilization. The fertile exchange of cultures— which can be seen again and again along the trade-routes and the pilgrims' routes—was considerably reinforced by the great crusading enterprises of the eleventh and twelfth centuries, in spite of their war-like character. This explains how Romanesque art in France, despite its variety, determined by the country's interior situation, could also show the imprint of the world-wide events of the day and had the capacity to absorb them.

FAITH

The tireless efforts of Emile Mâle and his pupils have shown us that, where this aspect of French Romanesque art is concerned, illuminated manuscripts and Oriental materials were important sources. Archaeologists like Marcel Aubert and Paul Deschamps and their fellow-workers have also established links—some of them remote—with foreign styles, and have been at pains to demonstrate how they reached their conclusions. The school of the art-historian Henri Focillon has made a special study of the Romanesque language of forms in France and its relationship to analogous forms of artistic expression; work which is being continued by his pupil and son-in-law Baltrusaitis. Increased attention will in future have to be given to the survival in Romanesque art of Graeco-Ligurian, Hellenistic, Celtic, Gallo-Roman and Germanic elements.

It is an immutable law, however, that the real artist can assimilate into the world of his imagination only the things that accord with his inmost urge, his own way of expression, that from the outset harmonize with his imaginative concepts and his shaping hand; in a word, the things that will fall on fertile soil in his mind and in his heart like the grain of corn in the Biblical parable. Only their spiritual readiness enabled the Romanesque sculptors and painters to create an independent, original art—not mere copies—from the models they encountered. The vivid tales of the Bible, the living doctrines of the Gospel, the pleading or praising lyricism of the Psalms, the visionary language of the prophets and of the Revelation were so familiar to them, that the already extant prototypes were at once vividly transformed in their mind. To summarize: The King as Judge with the four beasts of Ezekiel's vision (Plates 30, 57, 82, 100, 123, 133, 159, 191, 211, 217) is not some alien mystic figure; He is the coming Christ, the Christ of the

Apocalypse surrounded by the six-winged creatures, as they are described in the Old Testament. These represent all living creatures assembled before God's throne, and were symbolically assigned to the four Evangelists: the angel with the human face to St Matthew, the lion to St Mark, the ox to St Luke, and the eagle to St John. It is the same with the fabulous animals and monsters (Plates 140, 174, 178, 200, 201, 245, 246, 263, 270) of which we know much nowadays; for instance, that some of them are to be traced back through the Arabs and Persians to the Chaldeans, and were as a matter of course identified by the Romanesque sculptors with the monsters which frequently appear in the Bible and are invited by the psalmist to join with all creatures in praising the Lord. And is this Book of all books not itself full of Oriental ideas, and has it not become by daily reading an intrinsic part of the minds of those churchmen who stand at the artist's shoulder? Does not Jeremiah himself speak of those Chaldeans? Of course, they did not realize that their pictures were filled with a new, though related, imaginative content. We need only think of the confronting lions (Plate 265) to recall that thousands of years before they had been interpreted as the guardians of the Tree of Life—and now, with a branch still between them, they encircle a capital which serves as a holy water stoup (Plate 79). With an emotion extremely rare in a strictly scientific investigator, Emile Mâle wrote in this context: "On traverse un bourg rustique aux toits de chaume, on entre dans la petite église, et la première chose que l'on aperçoit, c'est l'arbre, gardé par des lions, qui s'élevait, il y a quarante siècles, devant un temple de la Chaldée." ("You walk through a village with thatched roofs, you enter the little church, and the first thing you see is the tree guarded by lions, the tree which stood forty centuries ago in front of a Chaldean temple.") A few miles farther on we find another lion whose splendid strength crushes the serpent of evil (Plate 80). And the same animal represents the evil power from which we pray the Lord to protect us: "*libera eas de ore leonis*"—those words are still included today in each Mass celebrated for the souls of the departed.

These few examples serve to introduce us to a world of faith which is no longer taken for granted, to a Romanesque world where the metaphysical is always and everywhere rendered perceptible, and where those who commissioned the artist, as well as the artist himself, were as much at home as in the material world of everyday. For their Credo speaks distinctly of God as the Creator "*visibilium omnium et invisibilium*". It is as consistent with the nature of the given task as with the inner vision of the artist that these invisible things should be made visible to the faithful. That is why everything represented on the tympana and on entire façades, on capitals and on painted walls and ceilings becomes a dramatic spectacle, in the course of which the ever-present angels descend from Heaven and the demons arise from Hell, to walk among living men. Not, however, on the three-zoned stage, as in the Gothic Mysteries or in the Baroque world-theatre, but unconcernedly and uniquely interwoven all on one and the same level. There is no specific "above" and "below"; on the central portal of Vézelay (Plate 33) a very human female juggler turns a somersault just above the head of the divine Saviour. The ordering is an inner one, and therefore often remains hidden from our modern eyes. The archangel Raphael, one of the seven who never leave the presence of God, joins Tobit and his dog (Plate 150) as a friendly companion, and not as the shining messenger of Heaven. And yet we sense his protective power over the youth; does not a hymn of the Middle Ages call him companion and helper who overpowers the Devil? Elsewhere an angel is shown in the guise of an armed warrior (Plate 53); for, as a matter of course, St Michael appears to the artist and the spectator of the twelfth century as the valiant knight with sword and shield who protects the righteous against the wicked. The Gospel Book, which brings the tidings of great joy to men, may be carried by an angel (Plate 120)— as on a neighbouring portal in this same region of the Pyrenees—or offered by a holy man (Plate 116); either presentation justifies the introductory words of the Book of Revelation. Thus, the inhabitants of Heaven and Earth appear marvellously related and united in their struggle against the powers of Hell.

There is, however, one thing that always puzzles us afresh: the apparent disorder in which this changeable world appears. Apart from a few sporadic exceptions, post-Romanesque art has accustomed us to a clear, comprehensible representation of theological doctrine. But in the Romanesque period faith has not yet been clarified by logically trained reasoning, has not yet been systematized by the tremendous intellectual achievements in the scholastic field. In the Romanesque period there is no awareness of the collective knowledge on which medieval Gothic thinking erected its philosophical-theological system of instruction. The Romanesque *summa* still entailed placing side by side, or one above the other—for the most part, indeed, intermingling—all things known or believed. This knowledge and this faith include much as yet taken on trust; and as there is no distinct line of demarcation—since revelation and experience can never be strictly separated—a great deal that is unexplored is to be found there. Man in the Romanesque period was without scepticism; he did not, for example, worry about the authenticity or the healing power of relics, and in all good faith he made his pilgrimage to venerate them. We cannot understand such an attitude; but it brings forth the faith that moves mountains, and that with years of immeasurable toil erects sacred buildings on the tops of mountains. The Romanesque style is concerned not so much with examining closely as with accumulating, not so much with distinguishing as with blending. The result is variety and abundance, or, seen from our own point of view, façades overladen with sculpture, walls overburdened by painting with a confused medley of motives.

This medley which has come down to us in stone was also offered in the sermons of the time. Daniel-Rops, who has made a special study of this aspect of ecclesiastical history, comes to the conclusion that "Instruction in the truths of religion was doubtless the aim, but nobody troubled about a methodical presentation. Generally the preacher strung together quotations from the Bible, interpretations of the Fathers, or even personal commentaries, allegories and anecdotes." The explanatory examples—*exempla*, which were never lacking—were taken from history, from everyday events, from legend and fable. Such sermons lasted for hours. We consider the judgment of the historian to be tinged with severity and irony, although he does appreciate and admire the vitality of these sermons. It is well known that their contents and their form exercised a lasting influence on Romanesque art.

In an essay on Jean de Fécamp, the most important "French" mystic of the eleventh century, Jean-Paul Bonnes reaches a similar conclusion. Jean de Fécamp, nephew of William of Volpiano, was born near Ravenna and wrote his Latin works in Saint-Bénigne at Dijon and later at Fécamp in Normandy. Bonnes speaks of "his *longueurs*, his digressions, his *détours* and his retrospects". He notes that this author takes Biblical quotations out of their context and uses them to apply to quite different things from those for which they were originally intended, that he upsets the sequence of Biblical verses, that he combines texts which have completely different origins, that he mixes up the Old with the New Testament and continually switches from one to the other. "But," says the psycho-analyst Bonnes quite rightly, "these are no faults in Jean de Fécamp, for they originate in the joy which he feels in speaking incessantly of God and to God".

Do not the scenes on the serried capitals in the aisles and cloisters or around the tympana show exactly the same, though to us they are quite illogical? Do we not see mingled here what we should like to have separated, and is not that separated which seems to belong together? One of the most difficult but also one of the most rewarding tasks for future research is likely to be the tracing of those hidden connections which may bring light to this darkness and order into this chaos. For to speak of "pure chance" does not explain anything. Confronted by these phenomena we must always bear in mind that the apparent freedom of fantasy which we interpret as an enviable freedom of imagination and expression may just as well be the result of a strict contemporary logic of historical association to which we have not the key. Where everything is so immediately experienced, so real and yet so rich in symbolic significance, where the senses and the heart are so fervently involved, there may be linking ideas, perhaps even subconscious ones—allusions in form and colours—which must be rediscovered. The most recent developments in modern art, such as Surrealism, might—in conjunction with psycho-analytic methods of research—open our eyes to these links. Let one example suffice to show how the sheer play of lines can in itself be of great importance, can evoke notions out of which images are evolved. The holy water stoup in the church of Farges (Plate 8) shows a grotesque mask evidently produced from an instinctive development of the partly geometrical, partly naturalistic ornaments which can be seen to the right and left in their original design and function. If the reader looks for it, he will find in this book a great many such transitions which, with surprising agility, cross and recross the frontier between concrete and abstract, because the artist is not even aware of the distinction, which only becomes valid at a much later date. A single shape can represent at one and the same time an oval, a leaf or an eye. From this point of view the demon with the leaf-face at Saint-Benoît-sur-Loire (Plate 227) is just as feasible as the head which grows out of a monster's tail at

Beaulieu (Plate 131). But since latent metamorphoses often lead to something fantastic or even degenerate into something scurrilous, they were regarded as unseemly and disturbing as early as the twelfth century. This is the period when the first creative artists who had become conscious of the boundless possibilities of representation were gradually replaced by those whose stronger spiritual discipline checked such copiousness and brought order out of chaos. How much more rational are the distinct rows of rigid, standing figures on the portal of Chartres (Plate 218) than the kings in the tympanum of Moissac (Plate 123) who sit close beside or on top of one another! Between these two works lie scarcely more than the decisive fifty years of the first half of the twelfth century.

St Bernard of Clairvaux belongs to this rationalizing generation. His dual attitude is indicative of the coming change. Looking back he rails at the overflowing imagination of Romanesque artists, which was unleashed once more in the cloister of Cluny. He is the moralist who condemns unmonastic magnificence, and at the same time he is the clear thinker for whom the fabulous beings on the capitals are so much dangerous nonsense. But as a theologian this same man remains fundamentally Romanesque. In 1140 the Abbot of Clairvaux was invited to attend the Council of Sens which was to legislate on Abelard's contested doctrine of the *Theologia Christiana*. Bernard of Clairvaux alone seemed a match for the shrewd dialectician around whom thousands of eager students were already crowding in Paris. Bernard interfered unwillingly in the dispute over the ideas of a man whose bold questing spirit placed him, even then, on the borderline of theological orthodoxy; but he was warned that silence might be dangerous. And so he came, but not for a discussion, not for a *disputatio* such as Abelard himself had introduced and now hoped to provoke in his own interest at Sens. Bernard came to deliver his verdict: supported by the Scriptures and the writings of the Fathers, he passed sentence on Abelard; not on the man, but on the philosopher. Here for the first time the pious man of God passed sentence on a rational expounder of God. "You misjudge, you disregard your own limitations, and in your intellectual mania you destroy the power of the Cross. Our faith is rooted in the power of God, not in the chimeras of our reasoning." Judgment could not have been pronounced more clearly. The Romanesque mysticism of the man at prayer stands opposed to the already Gothic scholasticism of the thinker. Over and above his great opponent, who is in advance of his time, Bernard fights instinctively against the coming danger of a reasoning, hair-splitting theology.

In the Romanesque period faith is not even discussed, much less destroyed by discussion; people simply believe. The whole of earthly existence is related to the hereafter, the natural is built into the supernatural. Our present-day outlook, in which—even where complete "dechristianization" has not meant substituting experimental science for the last remnants of faith—the supernatural is pushed further and further towards the borders of the natural, is so radically different that religion as an uninterrupted extension of earthly being into heavenly existence and an eternal flowing of the divine into the human is scarcely conceivable any longer. It is therefore misleading to speak of a medieval humanism, as Focillon did in all good faith, particularly in relation to the Romanesque. Of course, the humane outlook was infinitely furthered in the Middle Ages by the Christian religion. How otherwise could the barbarian who acknowledged only club-rule have become a civilized being? But the human laws were fashioned by a divine dispensation, and thus the natural world was upheld and preserved. For the sake of his eternal salvation man was also saved in this world. That is why throughout the Romanesque period the decisive attitude is the supplicating and thanksgiving gesture of the worshipper; this can be seen in the first groping attempts to give plastic form to the human figure, as represented by the praying men whose hands are lifted in praise and supplication (Plates 18, 68).

CONTRASTS

Far be it from us to wish to glorify the Romanesque period unduly and present it as ideal in the Christian sense. In the eleventh and twelfth centuries man, both as an individual and as a member of the community, was neither better nor worse than before or after. We must even confess that, as the feudal system grew into a valid social order, he continued for long to retain all the rough and brutal characteristics natural to a man who had to fight for his existence. History has given us sufficient proofs of the brutality with which the feudal lords asserted themselves and maintained their rule. The protection against external enemies which the stone-walled castles of the feudal lords provided for their peasants, who were at first serfs and who even later remained attached to the soil, was paid for by submission. Time and again the feudal oath was broken by rebellion. Even under Hugo Capet a revolt was fomented by the princes who elected him king. Henry I's right to the crown was disputed by his own brother who, for this purpose, allied himself with Robert the Devil of Normandy. But under this third Capet king the *treuga Dei* was introduced to check wars and the resulting famines. Together with the king's pardon the rebellious brother received the dukedom of Burgundy as fief. During the first third of the twelfth century Louis VI waged incessant war against rebellious vassals, and the Church gave him its moral support, while the growing towns offered him material help. Everything that, for good or ill, takes place on the highest level can be observed at the same time in all other strata of society.

In spite of their bitter feuds, kings and princes were the founders and protectors of most ecclesiastical communities. Called to order by the clergy, if necessary forced to atone, they were always ready to make good their misdeeds by founding a priory, donating land or making over rights and revenues. That, however, did not always restrain them from raiding and pillaging the monastery of some troublesome abbot. Such opposing interests clashed everywhere. They are faithfully reflected in the contrasts of Romanesque art, in the often horrific representation of some bloody event, which serves as an uncanny foil against which the fervour of the saints, the dignity of the kings, the solemnity of the apostles, the grace of the angels and the majesty of the Almighty stand out just as clearly as the new and mightily growing civilization stands out against the gloomy background of the struggles and wars of the day.

For civilization was everywhere on the upward path. It began in the abbeys and priories which despite external danger had remained the secret guardians of spiritual values since the Carolingian Renaissance. In that confused interval, it is true, the clergy had not been immune from the evils of the period. On the contrary, a continuous effort of reform had indeed been necessary in order to overcome the evil consequences of secularization, and of the deterioration of the clergy which did not even halt at the Holy See. In some cases bishops and abbots themselves became feudal lords, greedy for power and possession, who quarrelled over their worldly goods instead of attending to the spiritual welfare of the laymen in their care, instead of doing their duty as pastors and heads of their chapters and monasteries. Simony and Nicolaism—the material and moral depravity of the clergy—seriously prejudiced the reputation of priests and even of monks. These sad facts must at least be mentioned, as a measure of the depths from which during the course of the Romanesque period the Church and, above all, her administrators were raised—to attain new heights.

A powerful recall to order was needed to achieve this. Popes and bishops may have given warnings, but the decisive word was spoken, a living example furnished by Cluny. The Cluniac reform was a movement of mighty proportions: with indefatigable zeal it gave back to the distorted face of western Christianity its noblest features and, moreover, bestowed on it a new nobility, so that our historical conscience must accept it, once and for all, as one of the most important factors in the moulding of mankind. After the extinction of the Carolingian dynasty, and before the Capetian dynasty acquired power, Cluny was the only recognized ruling power in France. Much more is here at stake than the inevitable reversion to the spirit of the Benedictine rule, more than the renewed awareness of the true, apostolic mission of monasticism. Out of this dual heart-searching in which a few outstanding men of intellect and courage indulged, arose a cultural renewal comprehending all spheres of life, without which an over-all achievement such as is represented by Romanesque art would not have been possible. Of course, the movement was not restricted to the newly quickened spheres of purely spiritual and intellectual activities; from education to hygiene, from trade and transport to agriculture, from the Fine Arts to practical handicraft, there was no province at that time which did not experience this beneficial reform. Building and town-planning in particular were developed to meet the urgent demands of the steadily increasing peaceful population. The reform movement was not confined to the ever-increasing number of existing abbeys which accepted the new rule; Cluny also founded many new priories, as did Citeaux and Clairvaux later. These sprang up like mushrooms in the freshly tilled and cultivated soil; each priory at once became a centre of wisdom and of good deeds. To this day the history of the urban areas in France betrays the powerful impulse of this movement that influenced the Holy See and the princely palaces as forcibly as it did the bourgeois house and the peasant cottage. To this day on the outskirts of many towns stand sacred buildings, now parish churches, before whose gates the monks once preached. The Romanesque tower of a former priory still dominates countless villages whose population has gradually grown up around it. With an army of monks working quietly and strenuously, Cluny led developing France out of the smoking ruins of war, out of social chaos, out of moral depravity to new cultural heights. Could anyone who has seen the austere and yet mild Cluniac imprint stamped upon the French countryside fail to be touched to the heart? That the mother-monastery grew rich and mighty in the process, that by three separate stages it furnished itself with the greatest and most splendid church and the largest monastic buildings of its day drew no adverse comment until nearly two centuries later. By then another reform proved necessary, because times had changed, and once more the need was felt for a new spiritual impulse. It is significant for Romanesque art that its development in the French area fell within the compass of the two most important reform movements, both inspired by the Benedictine spirit. It began with Cluny and ended with Clairvaux.

It was not only the monasteries that, in increasing numbers, became focal points of a manifold intellectual activity, but the courts of the nobility, especially in the south, were also centres of well-ordered life, which was gladdened by the court jugglers and the music of strolling minstrels, and ennobled by the lyrics of the Troubadours. The heroic epic poems with their legendary figures from the first days of chivalry served as examples for the nobility. Roland at Roncesvalles, whose deeds, as we have recently discovered, were already praised in song by strolling minstrels in the first half of the eleventh century, and perhaps even before 1000 in Languedoc —Roland the faithful, who as leader of the rearguard of the army died for his king, and became the worldly prototype of manly virtues, as sanctioned by the Church. In the no less active sphere of the drama the popular mystery-plays turned a mere entertainment into a means of valuable instruction. From the secular jugglers (Plates 50, 177) to the sacred characters of the religious plays interpreting the Scriptures, all these *dramatis personae* also enter into Romanesque art. The parable of the Wise and the Foolish Virgins, of which there are many variations (Plates 102, 172), or the vivid scenes of women at the Sepulchre (Plates 146, 153) are widely represented in the sculpture of Toulouse and the Auvergne. In the characteristic details of its composition Romanesque art is nowhere detached from life, although it serves a religious ideal that in realization and teaching is predominantly monastic.

For all their love of solitude and their avowed principle of withdrawal from the world, the monks remained in the world; they were not hermits. In obedience to the Word of Christ in the Gospel they lived in the world; but were not of the world. Through the ecclesiastical duties they fulfilled, through the education they undertook, through their works of charity—in a word, through their social welfare work—they were in daily contact with reality. The content of the contemporary sermons often gives drastic proof of this.

It must be added that Romanesque art—at least in the surviving works—though exclusively a religious art or at least an art of religious inspiration, was in the main not created by the clergy themselves; its architects, painters and sculptors were nearly all laymen. The clergy gave the commissions, and most of what resulted was destined for use in religious worship, for the communities of the Orders and for the Chapters of the Cathedrals, even where houses or school-buildings were concerned, which without exception were built in the neighbourhood of the church. The abbeys and priories cluster so closely about the churches—without which they would not have existed—that together they form a compact whole.

The materials were taken as far as possible from neighbouring quarries, but where no suitable stone from which to make the carvings was available in the area, it had often to be brought from a long way off. In such cases we may find that the portal is made of a different stone from the wall into which it is built (Plate 82). We cannot here discuss all the various details of building technique; their study offers many interesting surprises. Suffice it to mention that sometimes the sculptures were carved in the quarry or in the builder's yard; in other cases the mason would give the final touches to the roughly hewn stone after it had been set in place. The first method is exemplified by numerous capitals which have one, more rarely two, of their carved sides facing the wall, or by columns with ornaments carved all around, as in the rich Bestiary of Saint-Christol from which we have chosen as illustration the base of one column (Plate 80), the engaged side of which remains invisible. Two subjects overlap on the three-portal façade of Saint-Gilles-du-Gard (Plate 94), though, admittedly, later overworking and subsequent rearranging must here be taken into account. The second and less common method is attested by the presence, next to finished capitals, of similar ones which are only roughly hewn, and never finished, though an ornamental or a figurative intent may be divined. In Mars-sur-Allier we find unadorned capitals of the same shape and dimensions standing at the side of the ones illustrated here, which may themselves lack the final touches (Plates 158, 160).

Certain passages in the chronicles prove that the monks acted as advisers or even themselves worked on the buildings. That they went into the quarries and stood by the artist as he worked can be deduced from the fact that here and there chapels, clearly intended for worship, have been preserved in the immediate neighbourhood of quarries far removed from any settlement. We reproduce one most instructive example: Saint-Gabriel (Plate 86), situated on a narrow, rocky headland between two quarries in the triangle between the important building centres of Tarascon, Montmajour and Arles. Though this chapel, built by a master, is not very spacious and is unadorned, it has, in contrast to other buildings in Provence, a profusely decorated façade with three oddly interlocking porches of different shape and workmanship, with two separate rows of earlier reliefs re-used to serve as tympana, and a gable also decorated with carvings. This profusion indicates that it was used as a wall on which the mason and sculptor could practise and experiment with different types of porches and in general try out various façade designs. How such carvings look in their finished state can be seen on the southern side-porch of Saint-Restitut—situated a little to the north of Saint-Gabriel—with its freedom and clarity of composition (Plate 72).

Now and again we find unfinished works, such as the relief-plaque of Notre-Dame-de-Salagon at Mane (Plate 73), which represents a hunting scene. The left-hand side, showing a presumably wounded stag in a thicket, was completed and provides an excellent example of the function of space-filling ornament to complement the figures. The right-hand side, a hunter with a falcon on his wrist, is clearly little more than a roughly incised preliminary carving, the drapery being barely sketched in. This relief illustrates a familiar scene of contemporary life—for hunting was not only a favourite pastime of the feudal nobility, but also a practical activity for the men of the Romanesque age. A medieval song begins with the words: "I trained a falcon for more than a year . . ." Naturally, too, there is a religious significance in this scene which is expressed in the figure of the stag. "As the hart panteth after the water brooks, so panteth my soul after thee, O God," we read in the 42nd Psalm, and mystics such as Jean de Fécamp, whom we have mentioned before, liked to revive the theme in their meditations and hymns. But for the layman, who had often heard it cited, there was nothing theoretical in this comparison: he at once visualized the deer on its way to the watering-place; for had he not often lain in wait for it himself? But he also knew that another greater hunter was always watching: Christ who—all unseen—waits for the soul of man.

If we proceed from the technique and the—often ambiguous—content of the works to their functional significance, we find again the strongest contrasts. On the one hand, we can easily see that purely practical considerations went to solve the given tasks. If stone vaulting is used in the shape of barrel, pointed and half-barrel vaults, in cross-vaults, with or without ribs, in domes of the most varied construction, it is an indication that these forms are being patiently tried out and constantly improved. And this can be traced back to the necessity of replacing the dangerous timber roof dating from the Carolingian age and continuing down to the eleventh century, which, if it did not actually cause fires in churches—wall-hangings near burning candles easily catch fire —yet fed them once they were started, with the result that the entire building was often burnt out and collapsed. But when, scarcely visible in the gloom of the domed vault, the symbols of the Evangelists are placed on the four squinches, they serve no practical purpose, their function is a purely spiritual one: high above the crossing they proclaim the message of the crucified Saviour.

In most churches on the left bank of the Rhône and on the hills of nearby Provence—in Saint-Paul-Trois-Chateaux, Saint-Restitut, Tarascon, Saint-Trinit, Saint-Michel-l'Observatoire, Le Thor, etc.—the main portals are placed at the south entrance, and there are no windows at all in the northern façade. This fact is easily explained if one remembers the cold force of the mistral which here sweeps across from the north-west. But the fact that the gables of those window-less and doorless walls are yet decorated with friezes can be attributed to an innate love of beauty and to a never stilled longing to adorn the House of the Lord.

In the same way, on a still higher plane, we find a purely artistic lavishness without any reference whatever to practical necessities. Statue-columns are set so high in the windows of towers as to be almost invisible, as, for instance, at Tournus in the north tower above the façade; exquisite detail is concealed in the topmost part of a steeple, as at La Charité-sur-Loire or at Nouvion-le-Vineux (Plate 242). Nowadays we can admire them with binoculars or photograph them with a telescopic lens, but in the twelfth century nobody could see them. How often have we not discovered with the aid of electric lamps masterpieces in concealed places inside churches, especially beneath the very high vaults of the Auvergne or at Toulouse! Why were carved capitals placed in the permanent darkness of porticoes?—we are thinking of Moissac (Plate 128); why place statues between windows against the light high above the choir?—we are thinking of Notre-Dame-de-la-Couture at Le Mans (Plate 260). Is this not completely senseless? On the contrary. They reveal to us the deepest, the ultimate and highest meaning of this art. Romanesque art is ever aware that beyond the human is the Divine presence. More than for our admiration Romanesque art is intended for the eyes of the angels, for the eyes of the Lord. It points to the unseen.

NOTES ON THE PLATES

The eternal—the divine—the invisible. Independently of one another the authors of this book have concluded their essays by pointing out the transcendentalism of the Romanesque spirit. The pictures show how Romanesque art gives visible human shape to the divine and expresses the eternal in the finite. Jean Roubier, our photographer, has devoted himself to the works of the architects, the sculptors and the painters, with a view to capturing the spirit of that epoch in monuments which have remained surprisingly alive. As often as possible he photographed the originals in natural daylight, even where necessary working in the dim light of the crypts. Only exceptionally, when a plaster-cast or a copy in the Musée des Monuments Français in Paris made a more distinct reproduction possible, was this rule broken. He wished to show the works of Romanesque art as the men of the eleventh and twelfth centuries saw them. At the same time, we must bear in mind that the appearance of Romanesque architecture today is not always free from restorations and undesirable additions, that sculptures have rarely preserved their original colour, that the original state of the wall- and ceiling-paintings is much impaired. The destructive hand of man has generally been more disastrous than the natural process of decay. But grandeur asserts itself even among ruins, and even the faded picture remains beautiful.

The problem of how to present the photographs has, after mature consideration, been solved in a manner which is in keeping with the Romanesque spirit. There could be no question of a chronological sequence; too many dates are uncertain and disputable. Nor does Romanesque style follow a logical development. Had a chronological sequence been attempted, some churches of which the building period extended, with interruptions, over almost two centuries —for instance, Charlieu (Plates 57–60)—would have had to be displayed on four different pages. Why not classify the pictures according to types, to parts of buildings, to motifs? But in a sequence of 271 pictures such a method would inevitably lead to a paralysing monotony. That is why we have selected in preference to all other solutions a natural division corresponding to the individual districts of France. In the text we frequently speak of the historically and geographically conditioned variety of Romanesque art, and, with reservations, of the "schools" in the various regions. The Romanesque was in fact not yet French in the national sense. Only the budding Gothic in the "domaine royal"—the royal tombs at Saint-Denis and the coronation cathedral at Reims—represents the style of a country unified under one dynasty. However, Romanesque art shows all the features of the individual regions out of which the face of France was only beginning to take shape.

So as to avoid too repetitive a pattern in the presentation of each region, variety has had to be introduced into the subdivision, too. The picture sequence is such as to simulate as far as possible an actual journey to all the monuments depicted, but it still allows certain deviations within the chosen framework. Added to this was the need to alternate general views with photographs of details, to bring out contrasts and to put on double pages items that are closely linked together (cf., for example, Plates 164, 165; 239, 240). In short, our pictures should come alive for the reader, who will readily be able to take in his stride a few knight's moves on the board.

The Romanesque age itself suggested the idea of a journey. The leading men of the time were far more often on the road than we imagine.

Romanesque art owes to those journeyings many of the impulses which continually fertilized and renewed it. Not only did they bring into touch with one another the various districts, but also the whole area of France with the neighbouring countries, and this furthered a mutual exchange of ideas. Besides the crusades, the pilgrimages in particular were of inestimable value towards this end. To allow a crime to be forgotten, or to enable guilty men to atone for their sins, the Church sent them travelling the pilgrims' routes for months, even for years. Others followed the same course in order to fulfil some vow. In both categories we find men of importance. They transmitted their impressions, and art frequently profited. In company with these pilgrims many artists, too, journeyed from quarry to building-yard. Sculptors from Languedoc worked on the west façade of Chartres, and the influence of the great art of the Ile-de-France can itself be perceived in the sculpture of Saint-Gilles-du-Gard, brought to the south by wandering clergy or apprentices. From west to east and *vice versa* there was a continuous give and take. French artists worked in Compostella at the "Portico de la Gloria" to honour St James. After their return through Spain, Mozarabic impressions appeared involuntarily in their work. We notice such influences on the heights of the Massif Central as well as on the banks of the Loire. The models, the spiritual ones of the sermons and mystical writings and the material ones of book illustrations, of textiles and every kind of minor art in ivory or metal, had long been available throughout Gaul, and in the Romanesque period they helped to shape the culture of the future France.

Our book is the result of many journeys over several years. The authors and the photographer travelled together, covering many thousands of kilometres, to visit the works of art of which they wished to present a comprehensive picture. Jean Roubier studied and wooed each individual work of art—often for hours or days on end—in order to get it to reveal its most impressive angle, its greatest beauty. To supplement his already considerable archives he has collected on these most recent journeys, especially for this volume, further pictures which enable us to recognize the essential characteristics of Romanesque art in little known works.

Our journey begins in the heart of the West, in Burgundy. No other province has for so long and so persistently preserved its individuality and its independence, despite an early and ever-renewed close attachment to the French ruling dynasty. Here we have a population that as early as the fourth century was in friendly contact with Rome and finally settled down to a Gallo-Roman culture, happily uniting "*Romania et Barbaricum*" under the aegis of the Christian faith. Situated between the valleys of the Loire, Seine and Saône-Rhône, the duchy commands the heights of an area crossed by many trade and travel routes. From the year 1000 to the latest phases of its style Romanesque buildings were erected here, each bearing the stamp of the personal genius of Burgundy.

By way of the Rhône, the ancient waterway of civilization, we reach the Mediterranean. Here and in Provence on the left bank and as far as the slopes of the Alps there was an intellectual tang in the very air; ever since the arrival of the sea-faring Greeks, half a millennium before the Roman invasion, the tendency had been towards urbanity. As a result of this unprecedented intermingling of tribes and peoples ancient art remained a living force, ever ready to be resurrected in stone. Thus Romanesque art, despite all its innovations, became here also a kind of Renaissance.

The Goths once traversed a latinized country, Languedoc, the fertile district under a genial sky, which for centuries had linked Italy to Spain. In these blessed regions cultural life had developed earlier and had become richer and more refined than in northern territories. Until the outbreak of the Albigensian wars, which destroyed the flower of civilization more thoroughly than any heresy, the castles of the South, especially of the

Counts of Toulouse, with numerous monasteries clustering round, were places where the Roman-Christian world assimilated and moulded Arabic-Islamic influences in a logical and artistic way. This assimilation is even more apparent in the Pyrenees, where between Languedoc and Catalonia in the small province of Roussillon, so rich in Romanesque works, a great art was evolved. The entire South remained faithful to Romanesque art until the end of the twelfth century; the Gothic architectural style already used by the barbarians of the North was regarded with distrust. Finally, in Béarn, where the Pyrenees slope down to the sea, the memory of Roland's heroic deeds and the crimes of the Saracens lingered on for a long time. Before crossing the mountains, the pilgrims who had come along the four great routes from all Christian countries met here.

Now let us continue our journey in the opposite direction: through Guyenne, the Rouergue and Velay the road curves all round the Massif Central with its southern slopes cleft by mountain-gorges, its windswept plateaux, its remote valleys where original Celtic characteristics survived longest in the country people. Here man is as rough and frugal as the soil. Nobody built as solidly as he. The churches of the Auvergne towering up into the sky have outlasted the centuries; their indestructible material defies the ravages of the climate. In the massive sculpture, with its underlying delicacy, we recognize the qualities of this race of men whose outward hardness is tempered by a rich inner life which makes them capable of fervent prayer.

Our circular tour next leads us, but this time from the South, into the neighbourhood of the Loire. In Berry, which is here encircled by the river, the artists drew their inspiration from ancient folk-lore.

Crossing to the other side of the river we enter Poitou, where Gallo-Roman tradition was accepted by the Christianized Franks. Here Merovingian sarcophagi encircle Romanesque sanctuaries. In Poitiers itself we traverse the centuries with ease; they unfold like the pages of a mighty book. Inside the town and around it, Romanesque art has conjured up really miraculous works of painting and sculpture. Proceeding westwards we come to the noblest façades erected in France before the birth of Gothic. Some of them are so rich that the eye can scarcely take in their sculptural decoration. Everywhere the limitations imposed on our selection of pictures has compelled us to make many sacrifices—nowhere more regretted than here. After a visit to the domed churches of ancient Aquitaine we skirt the ocean northward through Saintonge and find ourselves back again at the Loire.

At its lower course we enter the real "domaine royal". Bright Touraine, graceful Orléanais: all the contrasts which the vast area of France reveals, are gently blended here. We rejoice in the harmony of the colours on the church walls, in the harmonious structure of the towers, the height of which is not overwhelming. Before the royal portal of Chartres we experience the abundance of that age and admire the flowering of fully developed Romanesque art with its splendid foreshadowing of early Gothic. But we must go back! As we take a last stroll along the Loire to the abbey, where the mortal remains of St Benedict lie, the enigmatic figures of the early Romanesque period are conjured up once more in frightening contrast. Thereafter the Gothic style dominates in the Ile-de-France, changing everything imperceptibly. Nevertheless, in the shadow of its cathedrals the hall-marks of the Romanesque style endured unchanged in spite of the violent enthusiasm for the new style. They remained intact even in the midst of the battle-fields of Champagne and Picardy, across whose open plains invading armies have down to our own day poured into the basin of the Seine.

Following this river to its mouth, we reach Normandy, rich in pastures and shady trees. Long before the arrival of the Normans, after whom the region was later to be named, the Christian doctrine of salvation had reached this territory. Rouen, the most important trading-place on the ancient tin-route, was once actually the capital of a Roman province. Spiritual life radiated from such monasteries as Jumièges and Saint-Wandrille already at the time of the Merovingian dynasty. However, the men from the North had to settle down on the land and be converted before they were able—with the active encouragement of the Benedictines—to evolve the most monumental and characteristic type of Romanesque architecture. Right and left of the Seine, along the sea-shore, far in the interior of the country, and upon rocky islands near the coast, arose towered churches so huge that they justify the beautiful name of "God's Castles", which was invented for them in the Middle Ages. For the roofing of the interiors, which were as wide as they were high, the Normans, masters in the art of ship-building, used those wooden ceilings—some of which have been preserved—which rest on the walls like gigantic overturned boats. But all too often such roofs were destroyed by fire, and had to be replaced, already in Gothic times, by stone vaults. People were not unjustified in comparing the Romanesque Norman churches with the equally mighty edifices of Rhenish Romanesque architecture.

Within its present frontiers France harbours another group of Romanesque churches whose structure—historically and geographically conditioned—shows the characteristics of the Rhenish style. We chose them purposely as the final goal of our journey and so, too, as the end of this book. Lorraine and Alsace, the provinces of Eastern France, between the Vosges and the Rhine, form one of the most important frontier areas of the Occident—at what a terrible cost the inhabitants know only too well. The cultural exchange between East and West continues here to the present day in the lives of the inhabitants themselves; here history is for ever Now. In its essence and with its monuments the Romanesque art of Alsace touches a secret, which, once revealed and rightly understood, can explain the whole Romanesque style: in Alsace an often tragic, but always productive, and in its essentials a salutary encounter takes place between the Germanic world with its inexhaustible influx of new, youthful forces and the Latin world, whose everlasting cultural heritage is still a living force today. Did the two ever unite in a more beautiful way than in Romanesque art?

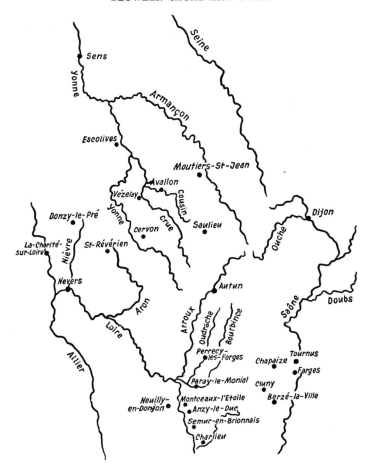

1 The former Benedictine Abbey of Saint-Philibert at Tournus is situated near one of the most ancient crossings of the Saône, in the neighbourhood of which prehistoric, Gallo-Roman and Burgundian finds have been made. The abbey was originally built over the tomb of the early Christian martyr Valerian, then it came to be occupied by monks from Noirmoutier fleeing with the mortal remains of St Philibert from the Norman invasion. The abbey was destroyed in the tenth century by another invasion—that of the Hungarians—and at the beginning of the eleventh century by fire. Several architectural periods, from the late Carolingian to the Gothic, can be distinguished, but in the main it is a Romanesque building with portions dating from the eleventh and twelfth centuries. The abbey was first consecrated on August 29, 1019, and in January 1120 a further consecration by Pope Calixtus II, who was staying at Cluny at that time, took place. Since 1953 the abbey has been the headquarters of the International Centre for Romanesque Research.

2 View from the former cloister on to the narthex—a real "westwork"—with its Lombard articulation of the wall (about 1000) showing at the right quite distinctly where the later nave (eleventh century) was added. The south tower has retained its original height and roofing; the north tower was enlarged and made higher towards the end of the eleventh century.

3 The central tower and part of the choir from the south (early twelfth century). Here for the first time the ambulatory appears in the form used at Cluny III, Paray-le-Monial, etc., and the great Benedictine abbeys built for the crowds of pilgrims.

4 The three-aisled ground-floor of the "westwork" is fortress-like in its massive structure.

5 The upper storey of the "westwork", the so-called St Michael's Chapel. The clerestory of the nave shows the gradation in the height of the aisles typical of a basilican structure.

6 Sculptures in the embrasure of the great centre window, which by virtue of its inscription is called the Arch of Gerlannus. From the nave of St Michael's Chapel it opened into the original church. (Today it is blocked by the organ.) These are probably fragments adapted from an older building (tenth century) destroyed by fire in 1006, for the capitals are too small in porportion.

7 The carving on the right in the Arch of Gerlannus, opposite the mask.

8 The holy water stoup in Saint-Barthélemy-de-Farges which is intimately related to Tournus, displays a mask formed by lines which correspond to the lines of the geometrical, plant-like ornament next to it.

9 The vaults of the nave and one of the aisles of Saint-Philibert at Tournus. The height of the transverse barrel-vaults and the beauty of the two-coloured archivolts show that early in the eleventh century elegant solutions to such structural problems were found.

10 The southern aisle with the wall which divides it from the "westwork". Next to the high inner double window some indication of the steps of a staircase are visible, which formerly led down from St Michael's Chapel into the aisles. Thus the pilgrims could walk from the crypt where they had worshipped the relics, through the side aisles into the upper storey of the "westwork", without disturbing the service in the choir or the congregation in the nave.

11 St Martin's Church at Chapaize, in the neighbourhood of Cluny, with its main apse, smaller apses, choir and pyramidal central tower, is one of the most harmonious buildings in this district (eleventh century).

12 Of the former abbey-church of Ss. Peter and Paul at Cluny—known as Cluny III (1088–1135) and once the greatest church of medieval Christendom—all that is left is this portion of the southern arm of the western transept (the church had two transepts), the octagonal tower, called the tower of the holy water, and the smaller one, called the clock-tower.

13, 14 The wealth of the carving which adorned Cluny III is evidenced by the capitals which originally crowned the columns round the choir. Today they are placed in the extant granary of the abbey in their original order. On the four sides of two of these capitals the eight modes of the Gregorian chant are represented by men and women playing music. The bearded lute-player represents the third, the dancing girl with the cymbal the second mode, as is clearly explained in the inscription.

15 On the four corners of another capital in the same series the rivers and trees of Paradise are represented. (These capitals were carved between 1113 and 1118.)

16, 17 The chapel of the former Cluniac grange of Berzé-la-Ville shows, especially in the choir, the most beautiful extant example of wall-painting inspired and encouraged by Cluny. Our plates show the martyrdom of St Lawrence and the monumental figure of Christ, nearly 13 ft. high, in the vault of the apse (painted between 1103 and 1109).

18 The capitals of the crypt, or more correctly of the lower church, of the former abbey of Saint-Bénigne at Dijon are among the most ancient remaining sculptures of early Romanesque art. The bearded man with his hands lifted in prayer (carved shortly after 1000) may be compared with the similar early Romanesque figure of a praying man at Cruas (Plate 68).

19 The once-famous Roman town Augustodunum, today Autun, played an important rôle as a bishop's see in the Middle Ages. The original Romanesque cathedral was adapted in late Gothic style in the fifteenth and sixteenth centuries, then modified again during the Baroque period; in the nineteenth century two towers were added to the western façade. Its Romanesque origins are nevertheless still indicated by its situation on a hill-top.

20 The tympanum above the west portal carved between 1130 and 1140 depicts the Last Judgment. It is one of the few Romanesque works of art to bear the artist's name: *Gislebertus hoc fecit*. The varying proportions of the figures are characteristic of the Romanesque style: the gigantic figure of Christ, the judge of the world, and the mighty angels and tall apostles, are in contrast to the small figures of the

resurrected dead being raised to heaven (on the left) or thrust into hell (on the right). A crusader and a pilgrim to St James' with his cockle-shell on the scrip can be seen on the lintel.

21 The capital shows Simon Magus precipitated into the deep like Icarus, watched on the left by St Peter with his keys and by a monk; on the right by a horned devil. This capital shows how in addition to the Gospel stories the legends of the Apocrypha also served as a source of inspiration (1120–30).

22 This fragment of the lintel of a former side-portal of the Cathedral (St Lazarus) at Autun, the famous "Eve of Autun", is part of a scene that was very popular in the Romanesque period: the Fall of Man. This representation of the woman reclining among foliage, of the devil's claws grasping the branch, of the furtive stealing of the apple with eyes averted, ranks among the highest achievements of Romanesque art in Burgundy (1120–30). Today it is in the Musée Rolin at Autun.

23 A capital from the cathedral at Autun representing the Flight into Egypt (1120–30). Paul Deschamps assumes that this scene is modelled on embroideries, and that the circles seen below the group of figures are knots of stuff translated into stone. On a corresponding capital in Saulieu the same motif takes the form of wheels under the hoofs of the ass.

24 Structure and articulation of the south wall of the nave of the Cathedral at Autun clearly reveal the influence of the Roman gates of Augustodunum, as a comparison will show.

25 This capital from the abbey-church of Moutiers-Saint-Jean (first half of twelfth century) represents the sacrifices of Cain and Abel, as explained by the inscription above the heads of the figures. The way in which an Oriental pattern—suggested by the material on which Abel's gift is offered—can be varied is evident from a comparison with Saint-Gilles-du-Gard (Plate 96). The original carving is today in the Fogg Museum, Cambridge, U.S.A.

26 A number of most magnificent capitals are preserved in the Church of Saint-Andoche at Saulieu. Some

of them depict the same themes as at Autun, but in a more vivid—we might even be tempted to say, in a wittier—way. The cock-fight is drawn from folk sources and is at once a symbol of the real battles of the age and of the eternal spiritual conflict.

27 At Saulieu the suicide of Judas shows how vividly Burgundian Romanesque art can elaborate a scene which is only intimated in the Gospels. These capitals were carved between 1115 and 1120.

28 The Baroque phase of late Romanesque art is magnificently represented on the portals of Avallon (middle of twelfth century). The corresponding smaller portal on the left was destroyed when the tower collapsed in 1633.

29 A statue-column representing a prophet, which has survived on the embrasure of the central portal; other figures were replaced by plain columns.

30 The figure of Christ with the four symbols of the Evangelists at Cervon (second quarter of twelfth century) shows how the influence of Languedoc penetrated northward beyond the Loire; but the posture of Christ is related to that of analogous figures at Autun and Vézelay (Plates 20, 33). In the border countries the regional schools intermingled.

31 Vézelay, on the summit of a hill, meeting-place of the pilgrims at the beginning of one of the routes to Santiago, is one of the most important holy places of western Christendom. The noble abbey safeguarded its independence alike against the bishops of Autun and the Dukes of Burgundy, and even against the mother-church of Cluny.

32 The basilica dedicated to St Mary Magdalen, though considerably damaged and badly restored, has retained much of the original work untouched; e.g. the south tower over the transept and the foundations of the monastic buildings.

33 Next to Autun, Vézelay is the Burgundian Romanesque church with the greatest wealth of sculpture. The main feature here is the very high central portal between the narthex, or perhaps more correctly the portico of the pilgrims' church, and the nave of the

main church. It represents the sending out of the Apostles. Between the Resurrection and the Ascension we are shown Christ appearing to the Disciples. "As the Father sent me, thus I send you. . . . Receive the Holy Ghost." All round, the peoples of the world—sometimes in fantastic shapes—wait for the Gospel tidings (1125–30).

34 From the wealth of the world-famous capitals at Vézelay we have chosen a scene from the Old Testament: Joseph accused by Potiphar's wife (1130–40).

35 Even in its ruined state the church of Donzy-le-Pré —really Saint-Martin-du-Pré at Donzy—preserves its former dignity.

36 The tympanum, with its carefully arranged empty areas, is still preserved above the restored lintel. The influence of Chartres is already evident in the Virgin enthroned under a baldachin between an angel scattering incense and the prophet Isaiah (middle of twelfth century).

37 The theme of Jacob's dream appears only rarely in Romanesque sculpture. This capital shows the sleeping patriarch and at his side the ladder of his dreams with one of the ascending and descending angels (middle of twelfth century).

38 The statue of St Thomas Becket (late twelfth century) was placed in the northern aisle (twelfth century) of the cathedral of Sens. Sculpture and architectural frame show the transition from the Romanesque to the earliest Gothic style.

39 The small narthex of the country church at Escolives on the Yonne shows that the Burgundian fondness for porches and entrance-halls, which served to shelter the faithful and the pilgrims, was not restricted to large abbey-churches. (There is no evidence that the original purpose of the narthex, to serve as a church for the Catechumens, continued in Romanesque times.)

40, 41 St Etienne (St Stephen), the church of a former Cluniac priory at Nevers, is one of the purest and best preserved Romanesque monuments of France (begun in 1063, consecrated in 1097). Here on the Loire the influences of Auvergne and of Burgundy combine.

The former is very evident in the central dome on squinches (cf. Plate 156) and in the choir (cf. Plates 144, 147, 149)—particularly when we consider that the tower of the crossing has lost much of its original height—and the latter in the articulation of the walls and the arrangement of the windows.

42, 43 The Church of Sainte-Croix (Holy Cross) at La Charité-sur-Loire was one of the greatest Cluniac priories of France, and, thanks to its position by the river-crossing and on the pilgrims' route between Burgundy and Berry, played an important rôle. At the west end, only one of the façade towers has survived, of the nave there are only the badly restored bays in front of the crossing and some parts of the triforium, now partly built into houses. However, the eastern part—the transept, central tower and choir with a wide ambulatory—still give an impressive idea of what this church once was.

The surviving tympana of the west façade provide examples of its carved ornamentation, which already show a relationship with the Portail Royal of Chartres. The part shown in the plates is today in the southern arm of the transept, and represents the Adoration of the Magi (first half of twelfth century).

44–6 The former Church of Notre-Dame—in 1875 it was raised to the status of Basilica of the Sacred Heart of Jesus—at Paray-le-Monial gives today on a rather smaller scale a very good idea of the architecture of Cluny III. Paray was a priory of Cluny and was built under its influence. The west front with its two towers dominating the small river Bourbince dates back to the eleventh century. The church proper was built in the first half of the twelfth century. The choir with its radiating chapels is a masterpiece of Burgundian Romanesque. Cluniac architecture is seen at its best in the high, beautifully articulated walls and in the choir, which, apart from the blind arcade, resembles that of Nevers (Plate 41), rising rhythmically over eight almost delicately slender columns.

47 A little farther south the tympanum of Montceaux-l'Etoile, containing an Ascension of Christ with upward-thrusting figures, derived from a Syrian model, testifies to the outstanding quality of the sculpture spreading from Cluny at that time.

48–51 In the immediate vicinity Anzy-le-Duc, founded as early as the ninth century and later attached to Cluny, provides, with its octagonal central tower, an earlier example of Burgundian architecture. A twelfth-century tympanum from Anzy is today in the Hiéron Museum at Paray: it represents Christ in a mandorla held by two angels, and on the lintel the Madonna nursing her child surrounded by saints. From among the more ancient capitals of Anzy (eleventh century) we have selected two which depict motifs very frequent in Romanesque art: an acrobat, and wrestlers, symbolically attended by two bearded monsters; both these popular pastimes are imbued with spiritual significance.

52, 53 According to Charles Oursel, connoisseur of Burgundian Romanesque art, the six-winged angel on the tympanum of Perrecy-les-Forges is superb. Christ is here seen enthroned above the scenes of His passion. Of the sculpture surviving in the wide porch at the base of the tower the fighting angel—probably St Michael—on the capital supporting the lintel on the right may be regarded as the most beautiful single figure. It shows high craftsmanship and dramatic power (*ca.* 1120).

54 From Neuilly-en-Donjon, situated on the left bank of the Loire but a part of the Brionnais, we select a small but impressive west portal (recently dated after 1130 by Oursel). On the tympanum we see, between four trumpeting angels, the Adoration of the three kings, which is the way the Wise Men of the East are always represented. A winged ox and a winged lion lie at the feet of the figures, an angel leans against the throne. (As the eagle is missing, the beasts are probably not the symbols of the Evangelists, but the monsters which the psalmist saw beneath Mary's feet: "*super aspidem et basilicum ambulabis, conculcabis leonem*

et draconem.") The lintel shows the Fall of Man and as atonement the washing and anointing of the feet of Jesus by Mary Magdalene.

55, 56 The architecture of Semur-en-Brionnais—the birthplace of St Hugh, Abbot of Cluny and patron of the building—blends power and elegance both in its general structure—particularly the recently renovated choir—as well as in details such as the balcony along the west wall. After the completion of Cluny III, towards the middle of the twelfth century, this type of architecture can be observed all along the right bank of the Loire.

57–60 Charlieu, situated near the confluence of the Sornin and the Loire, is the most southerly of all the great monuments of Burgundian Romanesque. Although all that is left of the choir and of the entire nave are the foundations, the abbey provides an instructive cross-section of Romanesque art. Founded in the ninth century and dedicated to Ss. Peter and Paul, it was at a very early date attached to Cluny, which determined that it should be reduced to a priory. Our pictures show a reincorporated relief from the first Carolingian building: Daniel in an attitude of prayer in the lions' den (Plate 59). The same motif in a double ornament (Plate 58) can be seen on one of the capitals of the extant arches of the nave (eleventh century). Plate 60 shows the double row of columns which originally stood between the two cloisters (eleventh century), and Plate 57 the tympanum from the northern side-entrance of the still extant two-storeyed narthex. It represents Christ in a mandorla, supported by two angels in the midst of the four symbols of the Evangelists, and is a typical example of late Burgundian Romanesque art (middle of twelfth century) with its positively Baroque-like profusion and animation (cf. Plates 28, 29).

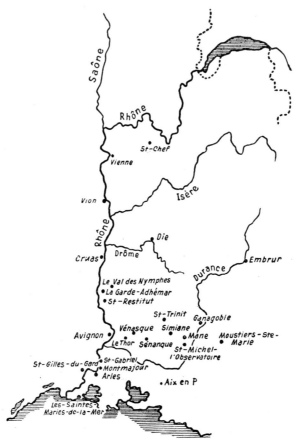

61 Vienne on the Rhône, the former capital of the Celtic Allobroges, was in ancient times and in the early Middle Ages one of the most important towns of Gaul. A temple, a theatre and other remains date from Gallo-Roman times. The early Christian Basilica of St Peter, today a Museum of Sculpture, was built when Vienne was the capital of the first Burgundian kingdom. The Gothic Cathedral of St Maurice still contains some Romanesque portions. The most important Romanesque building is Saint-André-le-Bas, once a great Benedictine abbey. Some sculpture in the church is signed and dated, a very rare occurrence: "*Willelmus Martini me fecit anno MILLCLII.*" The cloister (excavated in 1938), the most northerly in Provence, and the Museum of Christian Art attached to it, contain numerous Romanesque sculptures. Pre-Romanesque masonry is incorporated in the lowest section of the southern tower and the choir. The intermediate storeys of the tower, and the wall which raises the nave above the choir, were built about the middle of the twelfth century, the top storey of the tower as late as the thirteenth century.

62 The church of the former abbey of Saint-Chef in the Dauphiné, intimately connected with Vienne, contains in the upper storey of the northern arm of the transept a chapel in which has been preserved one of the most important series of Romanesque wall-paintings in France. Owing to its geographical situation it constitutes an important link with Italian wall-painting. In the western lunette of the ceiling the heavenly Jerusalem is represented, above it the Agnus Dei; on either side, one of the elect is being led in by an angel (*ca.* 1070).

63, 64 Almost without exception, human habitations along the Rhône are built on hills. Vion, whose church has unfortunately been drastically restored, is a case in point. On the early capitals of the crypt the character of the sculpture is something between an abstract geometrical design and a half star-like, half plant-like theme.

65 Later sculpture in the neighbourhood of Vienne, which combines the Provençal tendency towards

classicism with Burgundian originality, can be traced as far as Die in the Alps, where a capital in the west portal of the former cathedral shows Abraham's Sacrifice in a dynamic and dramatic representation (twelfth century). Plate 238 shows how the same subject is treated in the north.

66–8 The most important Romanesque building on the right bank of the Rhône below Lyon and above Saint-Gilles is to be found at Cruas. The abbey was founded in the ninth century; the building as it stands today dates from the eleventh century, with parts no older than the twelfth. On the floor of the apse is a Roman mosaic restored in 1955. L. Grodecki considers the wide transept and the plan of the two towers—the western one square, the central one round —to be due to the influence of Saxon Romanesque art (in what was once imperial territory). In the crypt —in reality a lower church lying beneath the choir and the transept—we find, on the other hand, the beginnings of a new, creative sculpture—in no sense representing Carolingian decadence—which though awkward in technique is bold in conception, striving tentatively for a new imagery in a territory where Goths and Burgundians once dwelt on Celtic soil. Among these first works of a developing art the place of honour must be given to the praying man with his large hands raised in supplication, carved on a capital the shape of which is merely outlined. Here we witness the beginnings of Romanesque art.

69, 70 In the case of the Church of La Garde-Adhémar one is struck no less by its situation, dominating the wide Tricastin plain on the left bank of the Rhône, than by its high, compact structure in which three east apses offset a west apse (twelfth century).

71 A little to the east, concealed in a hollow with a brook, lies the small, ruined church of Notre-Dame du Val-des-Nymphes. On a rock above it are traces of a Celtic Oppidum, and on the site itself fragments of a Roman sanctuary, while in the twelfth-century Romanesque building we find distinct Gallo-Roman features. This apse, completed rather late, may be compared with the early simplicity of the same type of structure at Vénasque (Plate 75).

72 The sheltered main south portal of Saint-Restitut (twelfth century) shows still more distinctly how all

along the Rhône the numerous Roman buildings served as models for the Romanesque style.

73 The considerably older west tower of Saint-Restitut is decorated inside and outside with reliefs forming friezes. In the priory of Notre-Dame-de-Salagon in Mane we found just such a relief with the partly finished hunting scene. This relief seems to be a copy in stone of a similar terra-cotta of the Merovingian or Burgundian period.

74 The foundations of the Cathedral of Vaison-la-Romaine—several times rebuilt before the late Romanesque period—consist of sections of Roman columns and capitals. Nearby, the excavated foundations of an older Merovingian apse can be seen. In creative ages the monuments of by-gone times are used for building material—not treasured as museum pieces.

75 There are several Early Christian baptisteries in Provence: at Fréjus, at Aix and at Riez. The four apses of the chapel at Vénasque, partly built into a rocky slope, contain a conglomeration of classical, Merovingian, Carolingian and Roman columns and capitals ranging over a period of a thousand years.

76 The Abbey of Sénanque (second half of twelfth century) lies in a remote mountain valley. The simple monastic structure is impressive evidence of the spread of Cistercian reform, even in the South. Silvacane and Le Thoronet in Provence also testify to this activity.

77 Saint-Trinit lies in the former territory of the Counts of Forcalquier, whose court was a centre of active cultural life in the twelfth century. Here minstrels and artists found a ready welcome and work. Nearly every village has preserved at least one Romanesque building. The polygonal apse of this recently restored church is typical of late Romanesque building methods in Provence.

78, 79 There was a Cluniac priory at Saint-Michel-l'Observatoire (the qualifying name was added quite recently after the Astro-physical Institute there). The situation of the church on a hill, the windowless north wall— the main entrance faces south—the absence of a transept, the elevated dome-bay in front of the choir, the south-eastern position of the tower—all these things are typical of Provence. (A restoration shortly to be undertaken will remove the entablature-like upper section of the tower, built of different masonry, and expose the pyramidal roof.) A marble capital used as a holy water stoup—it has two lions facing one another representing the guardians of the Tree of Life—derives, to judge by the style and the material, from the Roussillon; the Counts of Forcalquier used to be in constant touch with Catalonia.

80 Saint-Christol was a Benedictine abbey famous in the twelfth century. Only a Romanesque apse remains whose rich sculptural ornamentation forms a veritable Bestiary and Herbal with unusual and interesting details. Our plate shows the base of a column representing the fight between a lion—the power of good—and a serpent—the power of evil.

81 The former chapel of Simiane Castle is one of the most debatable monuments of Haute-Provence. The polygonal interior was to house a prince's tomb, the exterior is a round fortress (a later superstructure allows the light to penetrate through light shafts), notable in particular for the spiral structure of the twelve compartments of its vault (twelfth century).

82 The most important Cluniac priory on the Durance, Ganagobie—Saint Mayeul, Abbot of Cluny, was born at Valensole on the opposite bank—contains mosaics as paving for the apses (twelfth century). Unfortunately these are buried under the rubble of the choir. A partly restored cloister with fragments of the early eleventh-century monastic buildings now under restoration, and the nave of the church with the extant portal of the west façade still survive (probably eleventh century). Burgundian influence is apparent in the figure of Christ amid the four symbols of the Evangelists, flanked by two angels, above the apostles, single or in pairs, set in the arcade of the lintel. The Oriental cusping of the portal is unique in its shape and style.

83 The northern side-portal, known as "Le Réal" of the Cathedral of Notre-Dame at Embrun, is an ideal example of Lombardic individuality of style as manifested in Provence (end of twelfth century).

84 The Church of Moustiers-Sainte-Marie (a monastery founded in the fifth century) also shows Lombard influence. The nave is Romanesque (twelfth century), the choir Gothic.

85 The massive Church of Le Thor, which has not been appreciably altered since its completion in 1202, is a typical example of Provençal late Romanesque architecture. It consists of a nave with small west portal, a main south portal with porch and a polygonal apse; the bay in front is raised and covered with a dome on squinches ornamented with carvings.

86 The over-elaborate west façade of the masons' chapel of Saint-Gabriel (twelfth century) gives, like a design book, information about the working methods of the Romanesque artists. The various types of portals, the adaptation of older reliefs, the treatment of columns, the modification of ancient models, etc., are all to be seen here.

87 The old bridge over the Rhône at Avignon, Pont Saint-Bénézet, was built by the saint of that name, and the confraternity of bridge-builders which he founded, between 1177 and 1185 with money from alms received; its height was increased between 1234 and 1237. Of the twenty-two arches only four remain; on the second of these stands the Romanesque bridge-chapel, dedicated to St Nicolas, patron of boatmen.

88, 89 World-famous among Romanesque monuments is the former Benedictine Abbey of Montmajour. The monks of this house drained the vast marshy region between the Rhône and the foot-hills of the Alps, east of Arles. We show the choir of the church (middle of twelfth century) whose angular cubic structure is typical of Provençal architecture. The nave remained unfinished beyond the second bay. The watch-tower to the left was built in the fourteenth century. Farther to the left and partly hewn out of the rocky hill-side, St Peter's Chapel still survives (tenth century). It used to belong to a hermitage which existed before the abbey was built, and whose monks were the guardians of a nearby cemetery.

90-2 The Cathedral of Saint-Trophime at Arles is a late masterpiece of Provençal Romanesque style. Finer than the somewhat stereotyped carvings that characterize the friezes of the west portal, which was a later addition to the façade, are the remarkable sculptures of the cloister whose north and east galleries are Romanesque (second half of twelfth century). The corner pillars with their statues and reliefs (the stoning of St Stephen is shown in Plate 90), the capitals with scenes from the Old and New Testaments—for instance, the marvellously compact groups of saints —even the single brackets that support the vaults— notice the strength of the supporting ram (Plate 92) —all show a highly personal adaptation of antique models and the subordination of beautiful detail to the harmony of the whole.

93 More elegant still is the cloister on the south side of the Cathedral of Saint-Sauveur at Aix-en-Provence, for it is smaller and has no heavy vaulting (end of twelfth century). The columns are no longer set, as at Montmajour, Ganagobie, etc., in groups of twos, threes or fours beneath the archivolts, but stand freely side by side. Any monotony of effect that might have resulted is relieved by intermediate statue-columns.

94–6 Saint-Gilles-du-Gard, beyond the Rhône, once sited on a subsidiary arm of the river, has the greatest and most important façade in the south of France, with three porches in late Romanesque style. The original plan, a copy of a Roman triumphal arch, was modified under Northern influence from the Ile-de-France, and as a result the central friezes now lie higher than the side ones, and single columns with no supporting function stand in a rather detached manner in front of the façade, their ornamentation concealing earlier carvings on the walls behind. However, the whole impression remains one of strength. The sober statues of apostles and saints between the portals, whose relaxed attitudes recall classical forms, already foreshadow the Gothic style in the individuality of the heads. But the reliefs at the bases of the columns, adaptations in marble of Oriental textile patterns, are completely Romanesque, and so is the vivid Sacrifice of Cain and Abel (cf. Plate 25).

97 At Les-Saintes-Maries-de-la-Mer, where the legendary landing of the holy women, relatives and friends of Jesus is said to have taken place, still stands a simple Provençal Romanesque church built between 1150 and 1180—a nave with raised bays in front of the apse—which in the Gothic period was extended by the addition of two further bays in the original style, and fortified all round. Capitals of outstanding quality—unfortunately scarcely visible in the darkness —are contained in the apse of this pilgrims' church, forming the outermost link of the long chain of Rhône-Provençal sculpture. The crypt with the statue of St Sarah is the goal of the annual pilgrimage of the gypsies (May 24–25).

98 The former Benedictine Abbey of Saint-Guilhem-le-Désert was founded as early as the beginning of the ninth century by William, Duke of Aquitaine. It is situated in a remote gorge of the Verdus on the left bank of the Hérault. This abbey and a nearby village of the same name form one of the best preserved medieval settlements of France. Despite damage and additions, the church, with its nave dating from the eleventh century and its choir with three apses from the beginning of the twelfth century, remains the most important Romanesque monument on the southern pilgrims' route to Santiago between Saint-Gilles-du-Gard and Toulouse.

99–101 The former collegiate church, Saint-Sernin at Toulouse, is one of the largest surviving Romanesque churches in France. Saint-Sernin and Conques are the most representative examples of the pilgrims' church, a type with nave, four aisles and a wide ambulatory. Begun in 1060, consecrated in 1096, finished in the twelfth century (although the upper storeys of the central tower were built as late as the thirteenth), it represents in its interior and exterior sculptural ornamentation—in particular the southern

Porte Miégeville—an important example of early Romanesque sculpture in Languedoc. The figure of Christ with the four symbols of the Evangelists (Plate 100) is one of the seven great marble reliefs from the ambulatory (end of eleventh century). The articulation of the north wall and of the transept (Plate 99), and the view through the nave into the choir (Plate 101), give only an incomplete impression of the unique monumental quality which, despite all later additions, the Basilica of Saint-Sernin as a whole has preserved.

102–6 The former monastery of the Augustinian monks at Toulouse has become a museum—Musée des Augustins—and houses a most important collection of Southern French sculpture consisting mainly of the extant fragments of three former Toulousain cloisters —including that of Notre-Dame-de-la-Daurade—and shows the art of Languedoc at its height. Here the whole surface of the capital is covered by figure sculpture. In addition, the collection contains corner-pillars with figures of standing apostles—the crossed legs copied from illuminated manuscripts—and enthroned kings from the Old Testament (Plates 104,

105). The carving of a ship with oarsmen and helmsman (Plate 103) is valuable for the historical documentation it provides. On the capital depicting the Wise Virgins (a parable also popular in the Mystery Plays) these appear not with lamps but with stylized lilies, the symbol of purity (Plate 102); this is a suitable transformation of the oriental lamp, which the sculptor did not know. Frequently the bases of the columns also have carvings; an example is the ram-fight, beneath the capital with the eagles (Plate 106).

107 Very few Romanesque secular buildings have survived: a few houses at Cluny, one at Saint-Gilles-du-Gard. The façade of the Town Hall of Saint-Antonin, formerly the house of the Seigneur d'Archambault, gives a clear idea of such secular buildings: on the first floor the windows provide a colonnade for a large reception-room, on the second floor are three double windows, each with a central column, for three separate rooms. The carvings on the pillars of the colonnade show Solomon and the temptation of Adam and Eve, biblical subjects employed even on secular buildings (twelfth century).

108 The Mediterranean and Pyrenean province of the Roussillon, lying between Languedoc and Catalonia —and influenced by both—is a treasury of Romanesque monuments. Our selection starts with the so-called "Tribune"—probably once a porch—in the nave of the former Augustinian church at Serrabone. The marble carving above the fabulous creatures on the capitals is as monumental in its over-all effect as it is original in its manifold details (twelfth century).

109 In the choir of "La Mahut" Chapel of Saint-Martin-de-Fenouillar (eleventh century) are wall-paintings (middle of twelfth century) in the Catalonian Romanesque style. These scenes from the life of Mary (of which we show the Annunciation), from the childhood of Christ and from the Apocalypse, differ appreciably in colour and design from all other Romanesque wall-paintings on French soil.

110, 111 On the lintel of the church door of Saint-Genis-des-Fontaines is the oldest dated work of French Romanesque sculpture: according to the inscription it dates from the twenty-fourth year of Robert II's reign, i.e. 1020-1. The capital which serves as holy water stoup is more than a century later and typical of the art of the Roussillon with its love of fables.

112 Despite an elaborate restoration of the monastic buildings, Saint-Martin-du-Canigou remains an impressive example of a mountain monastery of Romanesque times. The church with the simple Lombardic articulation of its tower was begun in 1007 and consecrated in 1026. The drastically restored cloister retains, in its south gallery, original capitals with plant and animal motifs.

113 The Abbey of Saint-Michel-de-Cuxa, founded back in 878, formerly occupied by the Benedictines, today by the Cistercians, shows Mozarabic influence in the parts of the church which date from the tenth century. This so-called Lombard architecture is also apparent in the fortress-like tower to the right of the choir.

114, 115 To Saint-Bertrand-de-Comminges, built on the site of a pre-Christian Iberian settlement, belongs the Cathedral of Notre-Dame, one of the most important Romanesque buildings in the Pyrenees, erected by Bishop Bertrand de l'Isle-Jourdain at the beginning of the twelfth century. Three sides of the cloister overlooking the hilly countryside are also Romanesque. The rows of coupled marble columns are interspersed with pillars surrounded by statues. Sometimes the capitals combine plant-motifs with figure scenes; some stand out by reason of their plaited design (Plate 115).

116 On the jambs of the north side-portal of the Church of Saint-Just at Valcabrère (Valley of Goats) stand four great marble statues; they represent the ultimate perfection of Romanesque sculpture in the Pyrenees towards the end of the twelfth century. The capitals above the heads of the four saints—Helen, Stephen, Justus and Pastor—depict their respective martyrdoms.

117-19 The marble portal (twelfth century) of St Mary's Church at Oloron-Sainte-Marie, well protected by a porch, is iconographically and artistically important. In the upper portion of the tympanum is a

Descent from the Cross; below, flanked by lions, the persecuted and the triumphant Church are shown. In the archivolt the signs of the zodiac with the labours of the months, interspersed with fabulous beings, are encompassed by the kings of the Apocalypse (Plate 118). The central column, which supports the tympanum, rests on a pair of Moors—bound together by chains round body and feet —acting as Atlantids.

120, 121 Closely related to the preceding example is the church-portal of the former Cluniac priory of Sainte-Foy at Morlaas, until the twelfth century the capital of the county of Béarn. Oriental influence is perceptible in the angels on one of the corner capitals. The twenty-four elders of the Apocalypse are seated on the archivolt; they weigh heavily on a monk, with crossed legs and an agonized expression. The present sculptures are nineteenth-century reproductions.

122-9 St Peter's Church at Moissac—once that of a Benedictine abbey attached to Cluny—contains a number of important works of art, including Romanesque masterpieces. Most important is the great south portal of the narthex (which the monks fortified at the end of the twelfth century). In accordance with the Beatus Commentary on the Apocalypse, Christ is represented on the tympanum (*ca.* 1200) as the Sovereign of the World, with the four symbols of the Evangelists flanked by two tall angels and surrounded by the twenty-four kings. The lintel is modelled on a Gallo-Roman pattern; it has even been regarded as an incorporated piece of classical work. The six Apocalyptic lionesses appear on the front of the mullion. A figure of St Peter, particularly characteristic of Romanesque art in his attitude and gestures, stands on a vanquished monster against the left pillar. The elaborately framed left jamb of the portal (1125-30) shows, from left to right: below—Death as a devil, the Miser and the Libertine (Avaritia and Luxuria); in the centre—the Miser tortured in Hell (cf. Plate 152), the death of the Miser mourned by his wife; above—St Luke teaching and holding the scroll from which the parable is taken; Lazarus, the beggar in Abraham's bosom, the death of Lazarus, whose soul is carried to Heaven by an angel, the Feast of Dives—all according to the Gospel of St Luke (xvi.19ff.). The most outstanding among the six dozen magnificent capitals (*ca.* 1100) in the cloisters are the purely decorative ones with their characteristic tapering bases. From among the more decorative carvings in the dimly lit ground-floor portico of the narthex we choose the capital with the diagonally composed figure of the she-wolf carrying off her prey (twelfth century). The sculpture of Moissac set the course of the future development of Romanesque sculpture throughout Languedoc and far beyond it. The head of the figure of the prophet which stands against the mullion under the tympanum may serve as an example of this.

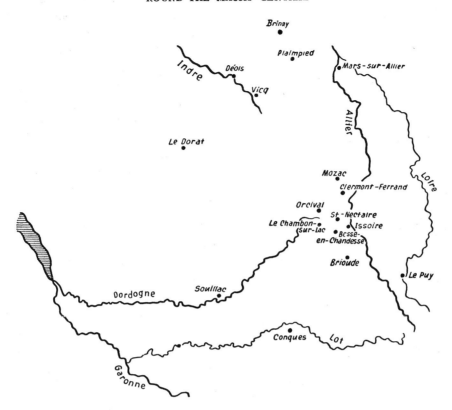

130 The figure of the prophet Isaiah (1130–40), with extraordinary twisted limbs and clothes, is closely related to the Moissac figures. This figure and other fragments of the original Romanesque portal of the former abbey-church of Sainte-Marie of Souillac (first third of twelfth century) are set in the rear wall of the present Baroque façade.

131, 132 The south portal (1130–40) of the church of the former Benedictine Abbey of Beaulieu on the Dordogne belongs to the same group; the merely superficial dissimilarity is the result of the different material used, namely, coarse-grained sandstone. In the representation—it is a formal composition—of the Last Judgment the outstretched arms of the Judge of the World and the large apparently asymmetric cross placed laterally behind him are striking. They symbolize the link between Christ's temporary life on earth and His coming at the end of time. An unusual feature is the double lintel with its row of monsters, Apocalyptic apparitions intermingled with visions of Hell. The elongated figure of a prophet as an Atlantid carved on the central pillar of the portal is also related to Moissac.

133 The Priory of Carennac began as a dependency of Beaulieu, but about 1050 it was directly attached to Cluny. The tympanum of the portal (according to M. Aubert it also dates from 1130–40, and certain of the figures do decidedly recall Moissac) adheres even more closely to the model and with its sharp-edged subdivisions seems like the translation into stone of a jewelled metal-work antipendium or an ivory tablet. Christ here appears with the four symbols of the Evangelists, between seated apostles. The work is signed: *Girbertus cementarius fecit istum portarium, benedicta sit anima eius.*

134–6 At Conques in the Rouergue on the Santiago route Le Puy–Moissac–Ostabat the spaciously planned pilgrims' church of Sainte-Foy, built between 1035 and 1200, still stands. Isolated in mountainous country, it represents with its high and narrow design—despite later alterations of the towers—one of the purest surviving Romanesque monuments of the eleventh century south of the Massif Central. The dome above the crossing—the squinches of which are decorated with the figures of angels—suffuses the lofty windowless nave and the central transept with light

(Plate 136). From the dramatic Last Judgment in the tympanum, which comprises eighty-four figures with explanatory texts on the framing bands, we reproduce a detail: Christ as judge (Plate 135). This work, which still shows traces of colour, retains some Languedocian features, but in style it is nearer to the Auvergne.

137-42 Le Puy-en-Velay, even today a much visited pilgrimage centre, was a holy town of France in the Middle Ages, and at the same time one of the starting-points —like Vézelay and Arles—of the pilgrims' route to Santiago. During the Romanesque period in particular a number of important monuments were erected here, whose striking situation is partly responsible for giving them a typically Romanesque aura. Foremost of these is the Church of Saint-Michel-d'Aiguilhe (cf. Mont St-Michel, Plate 247), which stands on the so-called Needle Rock and is reached by 250 steps hewn into the rock; another flight of steps leads up to the entrance. The façade (end of eleventh century) shows with unusual clarity the influence of Mozarabic art on Romanesque buildings along the pilgrims' route. The two sirens on the door-lintel (Plate 140) with their nets ready for the catch are the symbols of the dangers of concupiscence. The small nave is surrounded by an elliptical ambulatory (Plate 139) which contains capitals from the middle of the eleventh century moulded after antique patterns. The Cathedral of Notre-Dame, also situated on a steep hill above the town, had to be largely rebuilt in the nineteenth century, but has fortunately preserved some original Romanesque details (twelfth century); for instance, a few decorative capitals of rare artistic quality in the cloisters (Plate 141). Finally, at the foot of the rock of Saint-Michel-d'Aiguilhe stands the small octagonal sepulchral chapel of Saint-Clair, whose apse—a building in itself—also contains ornaments of Mozarabic origin from as late as the twelfth century (Plate 142).

143 The group of the Annunciation from Ydes (*ca.* 1160) shows distinctly how two figures separated by a column, even isolated in their niches, can yet be linked by a purely spiritual relationship.

144 The Church of Saint-Julien at Brioude, situated between Clermont and Le Puy, where a side-road runs into the pilgrims' route, finds us in the Auvergne, the heart of the Massif Central. In the structure of narthex and nave Saint-Julien certainly deviates from the classical type of church in the Auvergne and shows southern and Burgundian influences. However, the wide semicircular ambulatory with radiating chapels is characteristic of the Auvergnat style; this is brought out in the complete view of the apse in front of the high—not greatly projecting—transept with its central tower, whose octagonal section was rebuilt in the nineteenth century. (End of eleventh, beginning of twelfth century; cf. Plates 147, 149, 40.)

145, 146 Views of the southern aisle towards the narthex (left) and the nave (right) of the Church of Saint-Nectaire (first half of twelfth century) reveal an interior that shows the exceedingly solid and lofty architecture of the Auvergne, with a gallery above the aisles and open to the nave. In addition to purely decorative, somewhat heavy capitals Saint-Nectaire has, especially round the crossing and in the ambulatory, a number of capitals with scenes containing figures, e.g. the Three Holy Women with their jars of oil encountering the angel at the sepulchre (middle of twelfth century; cf. Plate 153).

147 Today the parish-church of St Paul, the church of the former Benedictine Abbey of Saint-Austremoine at Issoire—it was St Stremonius who brought Christianity to the Auvergne in the third century—is the most complete example of the powerful architectural style of the Auvergne. This is specially true of the eastern part, which, except for the rebuilt central tower, is in its original state. Note the reliefs with the signs of the zodiac above the windows of the apse and the lozenge pattern adorning the wall (twelfth century; cf. Plates 144, 149, 40).

148 The chapel of the cemetery of Chambon-sur-Lac, originally a mausoleum, is a rotunda, a type that was popular for baptism or as a burial chapel in the Romanesque period. On the façade is a mosaic-like decoration of polychrome stone, typical of the district (twelfth century).

149 The Church of Notre-Dame, built 1125-75, which belongs to the Benedictine priory of Orcival, has an Auvergnat choir and a high rectangular crossing

over the southern arm of the transept (in the interior a dome on squinches). Our photograph, taken from the south, shows a side view with interesting gradation.

150-2 The Church of Saint-André at Besse-en-Chandesse, though considerably spoiled by later additions, retains its Romanesque nave with a number of capitals which clarify our ideas of the early sculpture of the Auvergne. Our plates show: Tobit and his dog, ready to start on his journey, accompanied by the Archangel Raphael; the Crucifixion of the patron of the church, explained by the inscription; the Death of the Rich Man whose soul is received by three devils, while a serpent seizes his worldly goods. In spite of their archaic character M. Aubert attributes these capitals to the twelfth century, since art in the Auvergne is often very conservative.

153 As evidence of the harmonious composition the sculptors in this district could achieve as early as the first half of the twelfth century, we reproduce a dismantled capital with the Holy Women at the Sepulchre, from the ruined ambulatory—now almost at floor level in the nave—in the Church of St Peter at Mozac near Riom. Mozac was attached to Cluny as early as 1095 (cf. Plate 146).

154-6 Clermont, once the capital of the Celtic Arverni, where Vercingetorix defeated Caesar, has remained to the present day the heart of the Auvergne; it has borne the double name Clermont-Ferrand since the neighbouring town of Montferrand was united with it. The Church of Notre-Dame-du-Port—not to be confused with the Gothic Cathedral of Notre-Dame —was built on the site of the Ecclesia Portuensis, destroyed by the Normans in the ninth century. It was begun in 1099, continued throughout the twelfth century and completed at the beginning of the thirteenth, but despite this long period of construction, it is built throughout in the Auvergnat style. Plate 154 shows the south portal in front of the fourth bay: in the tympanum Christ appears with the four symbols of the Evangelists, flanked by seraphim whose three pairs of wings leave only their heads, hands and feet visible; on the lintel—note the shape of the gable—we see the Adoration of the Magi, who have left their horses behind them; the Presentation in the Temple and the Baptism in the Jordan with an

angel carrying Christ's garments. On the frame are explanatory inscriptions. Below, to the left and right, Isaiah and St John, above them, the Annunciation and the Nativity of Christ in very bad state of preservation (second half of twelfth century). Plate 155 shows the view from the nave to the choir; the crypt beneath has remained the goal of pilgrims to Notre-Dame-du-Port to the present day. Plate 156 conveys the impression of aspiring height even better than does the view into the central dome with the aisles rising above the crossing and the transept aisles. Beneath the squinches the flat corner-consoles used during the building have survived (cf. Plate 136).

157 The portal of Le Dorat, framed by polylobed cusping without any ornamental sculpture, shows Islamic influence. Such portals are characteristic of several churches of the Limousin and they lead us westward out of the Auvergne into the Marche. R. Crozet, indefatigable student of the Romanesque art that flourished in the area between the wide bend of the Loire and the ocean, has repeatedly drawn attention to the individuality of Limousin art and has emphasized the impact here of the Spanish Reconquista.

158-60 Proceeding north-eastward, we reach Mars-sur-Allier, almost at the junction of the Allier and the Loire. Its church, part of a Cluniac priory, is notable for some quite unusual mask-like carvings, not only in the tympanum—where we see Christ and the four symbols of the Evangelists accompanied by six apostles—but also on several capitals. They contain obscure allusions to music in the wind-instruments, some being also associated with the ears (Plate 158). The motif of Plate 160 is repeated with a slight variation on a capital in the nearby crypt of Saint-Parize.

161 Scarcely any Romanesque wall-paintings survive in the south of France, apart from the Roussillon. But as soon as we approach the middle course of the Loire, we again find them. The Church of Saint-Aignan at Brinay shows a cycle devoted to the child-hood of Jesus which is of exquisite refinement, especially in its subdued colours. The Three Magi appear twice on horseback, first on their way to the Child—the king in the centre points to the Star—and

then, below, on their return journey, which part we reproduce (shortly after middle of twelfth century).

162, 163 Vicq near Nohant is also in Berry. As in the church at Brinay, the choir and apse of St Martin's are covered with paintings. From among the numerous scenes in rich colours deriving from both Testaments and from the Apocryphal writings we chose a detail of Christ's Passion (Plate 162). It portrays in vivid detail the seizing of Christ. On the left is St Peter cutting off the ear of Malchus, behind them the hustling guards, then the tense scene of the kiss of Judas, and on the right the binding of Christ's hands. Plate 163 represents the scene in which Mary—according to the Protevangelium of James, Chapter 15—is accused by Annas the scribe of sinning with Joseph; beside and behind them we see the witnesses whom the priest has sent. This shows that the Apocryphal writings were also used as a source. On the right is an Annunciation (first third of twelfth century).

164, 165 Uniquely effective sculpture, characteristically dramatic in style, was produced in the area encompassed by the bend in the Loire between the Massif Central and Burgundy. Our Plate shows a carving on a capital in the former church of the Augustinians, Saint-Martin at Plaimpied. The pillar stands on the right of the nave, in front of the crossing, and the carving represents the third temptation of Christ (middle of twelfth century). On the same capital, rounded in shape like the column itself, a naked devil with a stone in his hand personifies Christ's first temptation.

166 The tower of the once great, now almost completely destroyed Abbey-Church of Saint-Gildas at Déols near Châteauroux on the pilgrims' route Vézelay-Limoges is a typical example of architecture in south-west Berry. This tower with its particular characteristic—four spires at the corners of the top storey—suggests Poitevin influence.

BETWEEN VIENNE, DORDOGNE AND THE OCEAN

167 Among the important Romanesque monuments of the town of Poitiers the Church of Saint-Hilaire-le-Grand, whose west façade and part of the nave were destroyed in 1590 by the collapse of the tower, has recently been very carefully restored, though with the omission of two bays. It is in more than one respect

an unique building. Three octagonal domes raised on squinches (top left in our illustration), which in the twelfth century replaced an earlier, wider timber roof, cover the nave. Supporting pillars were added to make the square ground-plan they necessitated. These narrow the nave, leaving a passage on either side with flying buttresses to the original wall. Since this church has also two aisles on each side, the pillars give it the appearance of a nave with six aisles. Our picture was taken from the greatly raised choir along the northern wall. The lowest storey of the tower in the angle of the nave and the northern arm of the transept contains some fine capitals of the eleventh century. The entrance can be seen, bottom right.

168, 169 Notre-Dame-la-Grande at Poitiers has the most richly decorated Romanesque façade in France; it shows clearly how indissolubly Romanesque sculpture is linked with architecture, and here (mid twelfth century) where tympana and embrasures have been left plain—the central tympanum is a later addition —the sculpture covers the upper façade. Individual scenes above the three portals are recognizable: (from left to right) Adam and Eve, Kings and Prophets of the Old Testament, the Annunciation, the Tree of Jesse, the Visitation, the Nativity of Christ, the Bathing of the Infant Christ and allegorical figures. Eight apostles are seated in the blind arcades above them, another four stand below the upper arcades, flanked by two bishops, Hilary and Martin. In the gable, Christ stands between the four symbols of the Evangelists. The church with its nave and two aisles but no transept (first half of twelfth century) has windows in the façade, the aisles and the ambulatory (some of which date from the end of eleventh century). The arcade-like form of the façade towers and of the top of the central tower is characteristic of the middle south-west and is repeated in the Lanterns of the Dead.

170 The late Gothic Church of Saint-Porchaire at Poitiers has retained its west tower (end of eleventh century); on the ground floor, which forms a porch, there are early capitals with inscriptions.

171, 172 The façade of the Church of Saint-Nicholas at Civray, one of the masterpieces of Poitou, is less profusely ornamented than is Notre-Dame-la-Grande at Poitiers but it is more harmonious in its articulation and in the distribution of its sculpture, whose details are of an incomparable dignity and discreet elegance. We illustrate a detail from the central window of the upper storey, which shows the various elements of these carvings: statues, heads of animals, foliage. In the archivolt of the central portal the Wise (Plate 172) and the Foolish Virgins stand, the one above the other on a curve (twelfth century).

173, 174 The church at Civaux, with a Merovingian cemetery containing numerous marble slabs alongside, has preserved fragments from the eleventh and even from the tenth century. The capitals with their traces of original painting show Romanesque sculpture in Poitou in its early stages. Above, the pilgrim taking leave; the husband and wife, already separated, are an example of the isolation of the individual figure even within the group. Below, a fabulous composite creature with hoofs on its hind legs and claws on its forelegs and the face of a bearded man, which is an example of the fantastic Romanesque metamorphoses.

175 As early as the reign of Charlemagne there was an abbey at Charroux, founded by the Count of Limoges. Consecrated in 1096, it once had a great central unit, a copy of the Church of the Holy Sepulchre in Jerusalem, between nave and choir; today only a fragment of the octagonal tower is left, the central portion, the two lower storeys of which with their arcades used to stand in the interior of the church.

176 There are two important Romanesque churches at Chauvigny: Notre-Dame in the lower town, and Saint-Pierre at the side of the citadel-like Château de Gouzon (eleventh century) crowning the upper town. We show the main apse of the choir ambulatory of the latter (twelfth century). On the wall facing the citadel the sculpture forms a harmonious pattern.

177-9 Saint-Pierre has, as we find so often in Poitou, a nave and two aisles of approximately equal height, which recalls a hall-church. In the interior, especially around the crossing, there are a number of noteworthy capitals, the colour of which has been faithfully restored. We show three examples from the various cycles of subjects of Romanesque sculpture: from the players' world comes a dancing animal-tamer, his "Siamese" double body emphasizing his movement and at the same time suggesting the realm of monsters from which the winged dragon below stems. The latter is one of the man-eating beasts expressing evil and sin. The Annunciation is purely religious, the angel is already pointing to the Cross; for the sake of clarity the Virgin Mary has her name inscribed in her halo. Several details testify to a keen observation, e.g. the flattening of the snaky curve of the dragon's body where it rests on the ground.

180 In churchyards in the south-west we sometimes find a so-called "Lantern of the Dead", from which a light used to shine over the graves at night. At Château-Larcher the lantern appears in the simplest form, a column of masonry with an interior staircase (twelfth century; cf. Plate 199).

181-6 Saint-Savin-sur-Gartempe is both from an architectural point of view, and particularly on account of its unique wall- and ceiling-paintings, one of the most important of all the monuments in the western Romanesque style. A Benedictine abbey founded there at the beginning of the ninth century by Charlemagne rapidly grew famous, and as early as the eleventh century a large church was built, now the biggest surviving church of that period in all France. The wide transept with central tower and eastern apses, the choir with its ambulatory and the two lower storeys of the square west tower date from the first half, while the three first bays beyond the western tower and the radiating apses date from the last quarter of the eleventh century. The other six bays as far as the transept and the upper storeys of the west tower were completed at the beginning of the twelfth century (the upper section of the tower dates from the fifteenth century). Stairs, passing through the porch, lead to the lofty nave, with its almost equally high aisles, which make Saint-Savin, too, resemble a hall-church. The roof-vaults at the far end, with no transverse ribs, are covered with paintings representing scenes from the Old Testament. Plate 185 shows the creation of the constellations: above fabulous plants, God, in the shape of Christ, hangs sun and moon into the sky. Below, partly visible, Adam and Eve accompanied by God and with the serpent.

Plate 186 shows Noah's Ark with pairs of human beings and animals above the victims of the Flood; Noah's raven flies over the bows. The two lower storeys of the west tower are also covered with paintings. The porch is devoted to Revelations. From this cycle we show a group of three inclining angels, one of four similar groups—making the sacred number twelve—of the heavenly Jerusalem (Apoc. xxi:12). Plate 184 offers an excellent example of the combination in Romanesque art of several scriptural passages in a single picture. As a vision of St John, the author of the Revelations, we see: the Ark of the Covenant appearing in the Temple (xi, 19); the woman crowned with twelve stars sitting on the moon (xii, 1); the dragon with seven heads and ten horns—"the old serpent called the devil or Satan", which seeks to swallow up the woman's child (xii, 2–4); the Angel seizing the child (xii, 5); the protective wings of the great eagle already hovering above the hard-pressed woman's head (xii, 14); the jet of water which the dragon spurts at the woman is swallowed up by the earth below (xii, 15, 16). The dating of the wall-paintings of Saint-Savin—which even cover the whole crypt—is one of the most disputed problems in the investigation of Romanesque art. A date between the end of the eleventh and the beginning of the twelfth century would seem most appropriate for the whole group. Emile Mâle suggested this as early as 1905.

187, 188 The Cathedral of Saint-Front at Périgueux is a building composed of two separate parts. Our picture of the exterior, taken from across the river Isle, shows on the left the modern tower rising above the older, so-called "Latin" church with nave and two aisles, which has preserved its façade of the tenth century; in the centre are five domes which rise in the form of a cross above the so-called "Byzantine" church (1120-50). The apse, seen on the right, is also new. Indeed, the entire structure had to be drastically restored. Even so, Saint-Front remains an excellent example of an Aquitanian church built in the form of a Greek cross (whose origin is discussed by Professor Gantner in his text). The view from the Latin porch into the domed interior is impressive.

189 We have deliberately inserted the simple village-church of Lichères on the Charente between the two

great cathedrals of Périgueux and Angoulême. In the simple clarity of its structure—seen here from the south-east—it testifies to the monumentality, even on a small scale, of the Romanesque style (eleventh-twelfth century).

190, 191 The Cathedral of St Peter at Angoulême, the ancient Roman city of Aquitania, is one of the finest domed churches of the Périgord type, dating from the eleventh and first half of the twelfth centuries. In the nineteenth century it was purged of later additions by Abadie and restored approximately to its original condition, as the east view shows: high central dome, a seven-storeyed tower on the north arm of the transept, choir with radiating apses and, above, blind arcades in pairs beneath relieving arches. The façade with its six dozen statues is one of the great integrated works of monumental sculpture. We show the central part: Christ with the widely spaced four symbols of the Evangelists, surrounded by hosts of angels, a master-piece of sculpture in the Poitevin style (second quarter of twelfth century).

192 Under the Romans, Saintes, once the capital of the Celtic Santones, became one of the richest towns of Aquitania. It has three Romanesque churches, one of which, Sainte-Marie-des-Dames, belonging to a convent founded in 1047, has a very beautiful façade of the Saintonge type; the carvings are here restricted to the vaults of the arcades and are especially rich in the archivolt of the main portal (middle of twelfth century).

193 The Church of Rioux (twelfth century) shows that here in the South, between Charente and Dordogne, even the apses display a rich, sometimes lace-like ornamentation which emphasizes the lines of the architecture.

194, 195 Aulnay-de-Saintonge possesses in the Church of Saint-Pierre-de-la-Tour (1119–35) one of the most splendid monuments of its kind. Our plates show: a porch-like arcade at the west façade with the crucifixion of St Peter in the tympanum and fabulous beasts intertwined on the capitals. The famous portal in the south arm of the transept shows still more distinctly how every stone, individually decorated, is nevertheless in harmony with the whole. On the

archivolt we see the kings of the Apocalypse with numerous fabulous creatures.

196 The extant parts of the originally Romanesque Church of Echillais (twelfth century) give an over-all impres-sion of a Saintonge façade with its preference for richly sculptured arcades. Although they conform, in principle, to such great examples as Saintes, the artists here strive for a characteristic expression of their own and usually achieve it.

197 At Melle, magnificently situated in Poitou, there are three Romanesque churches. From the wealth of detail they offer us we select—as a specially typical example—the radiating apses (first half of twelfth century) of the narrow choir-ambulatory of the former Benedictine priory of Saint-Hilaire, where ornamen-tation is restricted to the capitals and consoles.

198, 199 The tower of Fenioux (twelfth century), a conical spire on a square base rising above two round storeys of arcades, which in their turn are flanked by small, round spires—a rare duplication—forms a "lantern" and is the most elegant solution, between Poitou and Saintonge, of the problem of a tower-roof. This Fenioux also boasts a real "Lantern of the Dead" (Plate 199), which consists of a composite pillar of eleven columns with an interior staircase, an open round gallery and a pyramidal roof (twelfth century; cf. Plate 180). This is not the Fenioux in the Depart-ment of Deux-Sèvres, which also has a Romanesque church, but a place of the same name in the neigh-bouring Department of Charente-Maritime.

200 In the small, fortified town of Vouvant, situated on a curve of the small river Mer, stands the Romanesque church (eleventh–twelfth century), the double portal (twelfth century) of which at the arm of the transept contains important carvings. The great relieving arch, borne by Atlantids bending outwards, shows a number of fantastic creatures, some of which have human faces and animal ears.

201 Not far from Vouvant, at Foussais, strange, fabulous creatures are also carved on the Romanesque façade of the Church of Saint-Hilaire, among them a siren holding a bird and, below, a reptile in the usual shape of the "Tarasque" subdued by St Martha.

202 Through a two-storeyed narthex with early capitals (beginning of twelfth century)—note the animal relief at the base of a pillar—we enter the Church of Saint-Pierre at Airvault, which belonged to an abbey founded in the tenth century.

203 A large equestrian statue is sometimes to be seen on the façades of Romanesque churches in the middle south-west—the figure also occurs as a wall-painting, e.g. in the baptismal chapel of Saint-Jean at Poitiers. The statue actually represents Marcus Aurelius, but pilgrims to Rome mistook it for that of the Emperor Constantine. Sometimes at the feet of the statue a small figure crouches, which could well represent defeated paganism hurled to the ground, though some, interpreting the horseman as St Martin, believe it to be the beggar receiving a piece of the saint's cloak. Our example is from the façade of the former priory-church of Parthenay-le-Vieux (twelfth century).

204-6 The church of the former Benedictine Abbey of Saint-Jouin-de-Marnes, has one of the most harmonious façades in the south-west. In the gables we see the Last Judgment on single, slightly projecting plaques. Christ, His arms hanging limply, just taken down from the Cross which rises behind Him, is enthroned among angels above thirty much smaller human beings. Here, too, we see—on the left above the pair of supporting columns—an equestrian statue trampling a dragon underfoot, probably a St George, and as counterpart Samson overcoming the lion. Among the single statues of the Apostles, below, note the group of the Annunciation with its unusually slender figures. No less rich is the choir, especially its easternmost apse, the individual parts of which are covered with carvings. Yet, despite this attention to detail, the parts are always subordinated to the grandeur of the whole, which enthralls us by its magnificence and power (1120-50).

207 In the northernmost building of this almost inexhaustible series, the façade of Saint-Ménard at Thouars with the gallery above the portal and the side-arcades —depicting Christ with the four symbols of the Evangelists, flanked on either side by six Apostles— seem, in spite of unfortunate restoration, to foreshadow transverse galleries of the Gothic style (Notre-Dame, Paris). In the archivolt of the portal the representation of the Apocalypse is completed by that of the Kings, whose number here exceeds the original twenty-four (after 1150).

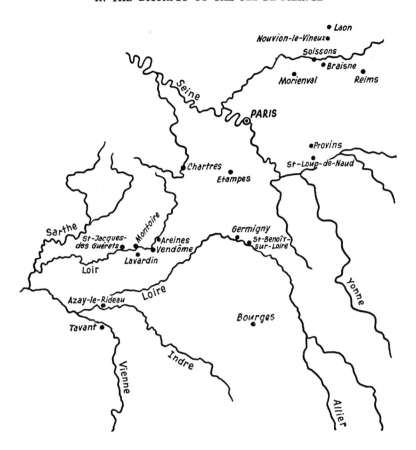

208 Tavant is situated near the most northerly route to Santiago, which leads from Flanders via Saint-Denis–Paris–Orleans–Tours to Poitiers. In the low crypt of its church the ceiling-paintings with pairs of biblical personages and allegorical figures inspired the pilgrims to meditation. On leaving the church the pilgrim saw, on the left-hand wall, his own likeness with staff and scrip. The palm-branch, too, is a pilgrim symbol. When climbing the Pyrenees all pilgrims set branches bound cross-wise in the ground at the top (before 1150).

209 Lavardin is likewise well known for its wall-paintings. But no less beautiful are the carvings in the Church of Saint-Genest, as seen on the base, shaft and capital of a column on an interior window-frame in the north aisle (twelfth century).

210 The west wall of the Church of Azay-le-Rideau is one of the oldest façades with sculpture. The

individual figures below the arcades—the Apostles with Christ in their midst—date from the early period of Romanesque sculpture (early eleventh century). The window, which was built-in later, has altered the original design.

211, 212 In the valley of the Loir we find a fairly large number of smaller churches whose wall-paintings show Romanesque art at its height. The chapel of the former priory of Saint-Gilles at Montoire occupies the first place. The three apses of the choir and the transept—the nave has been destroyed—contain representations of Christ. The most important is in the east apse: Christ sits in a double mandorla, surrounded by four angels and the four symbols of the Evangelists. Plate 212 shows in detail the eagle of St John with the Book in its claws and, below, the hand of Christ upraised in benediction between two angels full of life and grace (first quarter of twelfth century).

213 The head of a saint, moving in the simplicity of its linear treatment, comes from the same area; it adorns the jamb of a walled-up northern window in the choir of the church at Areines (after 1150).

214 How great scenes are interpreted in Romanesque painting in this area can be seen by the Crucifixion on the choir-wall of the Church of Saint-Jacques-des-Guérets. Above the strange green-and-black cross, sun and moon are about to veil their faces; below stand the sorrowing Virgin Mary and St John. Subject and manner of representation already foreshadow the transitional period from Romanesque to Gothic.

215 The former Romanesque Abbey Church of La Trinité (eleventh-twelfth century) at Vendôme is so hemmed in by houses that it was scarcely possible to take a photograph of the extant 262-feet-high west tower, beyond which the later Gothic building is visible. This tower is a little older than the much photographed Clocher Vieux of the west façade of Chartres; it is a fine example of a late Romanesque octagonal tower, tapering at the top, which, though still massive, already has a Gothic thrust (*ca.* 1150).

216-20 Some archaeologists, Marcel Aubert among them, regard the world-famous portal—Portail Royal—of the old west façade of Chartres Cathedral (between 1145 and 1160) as already early Gothic. Yet it fuses many single features, frequently foreshadowed in the south-west and fully developed ultimately in the Romanesque style, into an entity of unique grandeur and dignity (Plate 216); it was thus a valuable heritage for the new style that was just emerging. Our details elucidate the essential elements of which the whole is composed: in the centre of the tympanum of the middle portal we see Christ, the ruler of the world, in a mandorla surrounded by the four symbols of the Evangelists. The geometrical design formed by two circles intersecting at the margin symbolizes the divine and the human. As God the Father is represented in human shape (Plate 217), Daniel-Rops was justified in calling this portal "le porche du Dieu vivant", the portal of the living God. The figures from the ancient Covenant on the columns of the intrados give to the Gospel events, depicted above, their royal foundation and show at the same time the human ancestors of Mary, Mother of Christ, who is

seen in the right tympanum. One figure only is still Romanesque, hieratically sublime and at the same time Gothic and beautifully human (Plate 219). In the left tympanum we see the Ascension of Christ, which is announced to the Apostles on the lintel below by angels flying down to earth. These scenes are already clearly arranged, one above the other, by separating lines in Gothic gradation (cf. Moissac, Plate 123).

221 The influence of the Portail Royal as a bridge between Romanesque and Gothic was felt as far afield as Burgundy and Provence, and, of course, more directly in the Ile-de-France. As an example of this we have selected the south portal of Notre-Dame at Etampes, which despite its damaged condition remains magnificent. As at Chartres, the statues of the jambs are not yet stereotyped at a uniform height (*ca.* 1150).

222 The Gothic form of the tympanum, in which horizontal strips are set one above the other, was already foreshadowed in the Romanesque style—as can be seen in that of Saint-Ursin at Bourges—at number 28 of the Avenue Henri-Ducrot. Here, ranged one above the other beneath arcades, are the months with their seasonal labours, a hunt in a sequence of episodes and four fabulous scenes. The work, which M. Aubert and P. Deschamps date as belonging to the end of the eleventh century, is signed: *Girauldus fecit istas portas.*

223 Within its thirteenth-century porticoes the Gothic Cathedral of St Stephen at Bourges still retains its late Romanesque side-portals; the southern one is especially well preserved. We show a section of the zone of capitals above the statue-columns and the beginning of the archivolt, the whole of which bears carvings (middle of twelfth century). The influence of Chartres is also noticeable here.

224-30 On the right bank of the river, above Orléans, lies Saint-Benoît-sur-Loire. In the Middle Ages this was one of the greatest Benedictine abbeys, built like Chartres on the site of a former Druid sanctuary. It was founded in the middle of the seventh century under its original name of Fleury. But in the same century the mortal remains of St Benedict were rescued and brought to this abbey from Monte Cassino, which had been destroyed by the Lombards.

Fleury, under its new name of Saint-Benoît, became a great pilgrimage centre, and the monastery famous for its school. Alongside the new monastic buildings the old church remained, parts of which date from the eleventh, twelfth and the beginning of the thirteenth centuries (there are later additions and restorations). The south view (Plate 225) shows the clean structure of a tower-like porch with an open portico—often called a narthex—on the ground floor, the high nave flanked by two low aisles, the strongly projecting transept, the square central tower, the extended choir with ambulatory and radiating chapels (which is interrupted by the Gothic annexe). This is the typical Benedictine abbey-church with plenty of space for the many monks, as we can see from the lofty choir with its raised altar standing above the crypt (Plate 226; last third of eleventh century) and with blind arcades below the clerestory. Much in this church is intended specially for the pilgrims, particularly the many capitals, which are distributed over the two storeys of the west tower and through the whole building to the choir, and on which purely ornamental decoration alternates with many instructive scenes with figures. They give a lively conspectus of Romanesque imagery. Our selection, taken from the portico, shows the human soul as an infant between a cherub and a leaf-faced devil, thus clearly characterizing the position of the Christian. The figures are still half adapted to the original form of the foliated capital (Plate 227). The earliest capital, showing several standing and reclining figures which have not yet been interpreted, was originally on a south-eastern pillar in the crossing. It recalls in many particulars very early Germanic times, and is also an example of the first Romanesque attempt to give plastic form to the human figure (Plate 228). The partly restored capital with the three heads, which presumably represent the three Magi (Plate 229), has also been dismantled because of its damaged condition. The crypt, like these carvings, dates from the eleventh century, though it was restored in the nineteenth century. The mortal remains of St Benedict are in the central martyrium. The mosaics in the choir (fourth–fifth century) were brought from Italy to Saint-Benoît as late as the sixteenth century. The important north side-portal is Gothic (thirteenth century).

231 The Carolingian Church of Germigny-des-Prés (now completely rebuilt in its original style) stands near Saint-Benoît and was once dependent on it. The nave, which was added later, houses a baptismal font, the front of which is decorated with a relief representing the Baptism of Christ. At the top, left, we see the hand of God with its three outstretched fingers pointing to the Son (eleventh century).

232 The central pillar of the portal and the statues on the left wall of the porch of Saint-Loup-de-Naud, church of a former Benedictine priory, once dependent on Saint-Pierre at Sens, show Burgundian influence and with increasing clarity the transition to the Gothic style (1170–80). On the central pillar: the patron of the church; on the capital above him: a miracle which he performed; on the wall: the Apostle Paul with the Book, the Queen of Sheba and a patriarch.

233 Most of the Romanesque citadels were destroyed or rebuilt in Gothic times. The so-called Tower of Caesar, at Provins, genuine and well preserved—apart from the restored roof—shows the octagonal structure of a twelfth-century fortress (it was known before 1137).

234 There were several Romanesque buildings in Paris, nearly all of which fell victim to later rebuilding. There still remain Saint-Germain-des-Prés—drastically restored—and Saint-Pierre-de-Montmartre, the most ancient portions of which are Romanesque. We show the eastern part, with a double ambulatory, of the choir (1130–40) and the south tower of the former Cluniac priory church of Saint-Martin-des-Champs, once, as its name implies, situated in fields outside the gates. Today it is used as an industrial museum.

235, 236 Though Gothic art predominates here, important Romanesque buildings were previously erected to the north of Paris, such as the abbey-church of the Benedictine nuns, Notre-Dame-de-Morienval. Built in the eleventh century and enlarged about 1130 by the addition of an ambulatory to the choir, it shows the earliest form of Gothic vaulting. The two towers between transept and choir are authentic, as well as the original stone-roofing. The church has been drastically restored, but some original capitals in the interior testify to the somewhat clumsy but impressive and massive sculpture of the eleventh century (Plate 236).

237, 238 The vigorous and at the same time elegant form of Romanesque art in the Ile-de-France is shown in the capital chosen from the former Abbey-Church of

Saint-Médard of Soissons, today in the museum, the former Abbey of Saint-Léger. It represents the Sacrifice of Abraham: at the top, the patriarch sets out with his son, the wood for the altar serving as a saddle for Isaac; below, an angel stays the father's uplifted sword, and at the same time points to the ram that is to be sacrificed; on the right Isaac sits with his face turned away (twelfth century; cf. Plate 65).

239, 240 Just as we showed some pre-Romanesque works as an introduction to our subject, we have chosen two large figures, part of a Coronation of the Virgin from the former portal of the Church of Saint-Yved at Braisne—now placed separately in the choir of the restored church—to illustrate the further development of late Romanesque sculpture to the threshold of the early Gothic style. Behind Mary we see fragments of the figure of an angel burning incense (ca. 1200).

241 Behind the Gothic cathedral of Laon stands the Chapel of the Knights Templars—a rotunda, a small choir and an apse forming a beautiful whole and testifying to the high accomplishment of Romanesque architects in Picardy (middle of twelfth century).

242 At Bruyères, too, there is a Romanesque church with a richly decorated choir, and a little south of Laon, above the village of Nouvion-le-Vineux, rises the most beautiful and best preserved Romanesque tower of the area, as astonishing in its total effect—achieved by the happy proportions of the storeys—as it is fascinating in the details of the sculptural ornamentation of its windows (twelfth century).

243-6 Champagne has its Romanesque buildings, too, such as the Abbey-Church of Saint-Rémi at Reims whose great twelfth-century nave has been preserved, although the Gothic eastern part was recently severely damaged. After being walled-up for centuries, a number of slender capitals were recently discovered by chance in the ruins of the former abbey. Romanesque survivors, marvellously fresh and untouched, they have been boldly incorporated into the Gothic arcades. We choose from among them two purely ornamental capitals and two others on which are seen a shaggy, bearded creature and an owl perched among branches, behind which a similar bird with an almost human face appears in profile (twelfth century).

NORMANDY AND MAINE

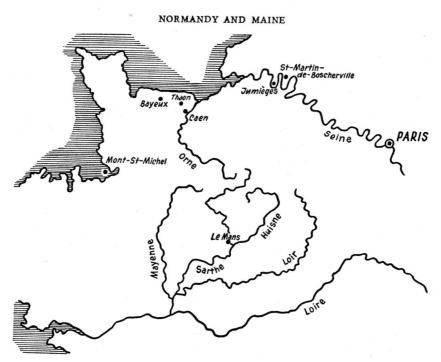

247, 248 In the bay where Normandy and Brittany meet, a granite rock swept by the tides towers off the coast. In Celtic times an island of the dead, Mont Tombe,

it has since the eighth century been crowned by a small Christian sanctuary, which was adapted as a Carolingian church, Notre-Dame-sous-Terre, in the tenth century. The foundations of the later building, i.e. the Romanesque abbey, were partly rebuilt in Gothic times, in particular the choir and the monastic buildings (fifteenth century). Finally a fishing village was built at the foot of the monastic settlement, called Mont Saint-Michel-au-Péril-de-la-Mer. The Romanesque nave, the transept and the central tower (1022–1135) still survive. The interior of the nave (Plate 248) shows the typical Norman articulation of the walls with a particularly beautiful triforium and the clerestory above, which has remained unchanged—a rarity, for the original timber ceiling (top left) has not been replaced by Gothic vaulting as it has in other churches in Normandy.

249–53 William, called the Bastard, later the Conqueror, and his wife Matilda, despite their near relationship, married without first obtaining a dispensation from the Pope. To atone for this they founded two abbeys in Caen in 1062—she La Trinité or Abbaye aux Dames (Plates 249, 250), he Saint-Etienne or Abbaye aux Hommes. Their churches have remained intact in spite of recent heavy damage to the town. Of the former we show the massive west façade with a view of the nave and the central tower (eleventh century, except for top storey of the façade towers, seventeenth century) as well as the articulation in the interior of the transept which was later altered when a Gothic vault was constructed over the upper part above the triforium. Quite different is the second type of articulated Norman wall, to be seen in the nave of Saint-Etienne (Plate 251) with its wide and lofty gallery arcades above the aisles. Here, too, the fenestration was transformed by the Gothic vaulting. The balustrade is seventeenth-century "Gothic". Saint-Etienne was consecrated in 1077. The exterior was transformed in post-Romanesque times. Nevertheless, the view from the south-east (Plate 252) still clearly shows the Romanesque structure with its many towers; the top storey and the summit of the façade towers are in the best Norman Gothic tradition (thirteenth century), and represent a natural development. Only the compact central tower above the great crossing is of more recent date. In 1083 the Benedictine monks had the Church of Saint-Nicolas, not far from their abbey, built for their vassals. It has remained almost unchanged since the end of the eleventh century. The choir-apse with its slender

engaged columns is a further example of sober Norman elegance (Plate 253).

254 The church of the former leper house of Thaon in the valley of the tiny river Mue shows how delightful Norman architecture can be also in smaller buildings. The original aisles, it is true, have disappeared, and for that reason the nave has been walled in. The severe, flat choir-apse is in contrast to the refined ornamentation of the Norman arches, especially those of the central tower.

255 The Cathedral of Notre-Dame at Bayeux is one of those great buildings which, Romanesque in structure, were wholly restored, or at least transformed, in Gothic times. However, this cathedral has preserved individual, purely Romanesque portions in which we recognize the original beauty of the building; for instance, in the nave between Gothic cusped capitals and Gothic triforium, the original portion of the arcades with their varied, geometrical patterns and the typical Norman wall-decoration in the form of a plaited band. The reliefs in the spandrels suggest Irish or perhaps Asiatic influence.

256 The towering ruins of the Abbey-Church of Notre-Dame at Jumièges, situated in a bend of the Seine, testify to the grandeur and splendour of one of the most important works of Norman Romanesque art. The eastern part was restored in Gothic times and finally destroyed, but the view from what remains of the crossing through the nave (1052–67) to one of the façade towers gives us an idea of the magnitude of the loss. Note the articulation of the wall, especially the alternating supports and the extreme height of the clerestory.

257 Behind Saint-Martin-de-Boscherville, upstream, on another curve of the Seine, stands the well-preserved abbey-church dedicated to St George. Compared with other churches, the west façade, completed only in the thirteenth century, is somewhat weak. The eastern part is far more beautiful, its projecting transept with eastern apses, mighty central tower, choir with aisles and high apse forming an impressive whole (completed 1125).

258, 259 In the Romanesque part of the Cathedral of Saint-Julien at Le Mans influences from South and North meet. The statues on the wall of the south portal show a connection with Chartres, but lack the rhythmic grace of the Portail Royal (cf. Plate 218). The original timber roofing of the nave, twice burnt down, was finally replaced by Gothic vaulting; the walls show typical Norman articulation with alternating supports. The twelfth-century structure built in below the eleventh-century Norman arch should be noted (completed 1154).

260 Parts of Notre-Dame-de-la-Couture at Le Mans are much older than the cathedral. At the lower end of the ambulatory the choir—which now has Gothic vaulting—testifies to the power of the Early Romanesque style in the eleventh century. Particularly notable are the six statues in the so-called Plantagenet style with their slight inward curve, which stand between the choir-windows below the base of the vault (twelfth century). These are typical of the West, where, until the victory of Bouvines (1214), the kings of England reigned.

FROM THE VOSGES TO THE RHINE

261 Pompierre, in Joan of Arc's country, where few Romanesque buildings have been preserved, still retains the old portal in its new church. Decorative carvings revealing the influence of nearby Burgundy are harmoniously distributed over bases, columns, capitals and especially the archivolt. Tympanum and lintel tell of events in the life of Christ: in the centre, the happy tidings brought to the shepherds and the Adoration of the Magi; at the top, the Massacre of the Innocents in Bethlehem and the Flight into Egypt; below, the Virgin standing with the Child and the Entry into Jerusalem. Crouching Atlantids support the lintel (twelfth century).

262 In Alsace we enter another province of Romanesque art, where building was in the Rhenish style. The façade of the Church of Sainte-Foy at Sélestat does not show the in other respects typical Lombard wall-decoration to be seen, say, in Marmoutier and Guebwiller; the influence of Lorraine is noticeable in the attractive ornamentation of the arcading and the delicate engaged columns (resembling those at Notre-Dame at Saint-Dié). But the two towers with their windowless lower storeys and the porch with the upper storey severely articulated constitute a genuine "westwork" (second half of twelfth century). Nave-gable and tower roofing are unfortunately new.

263, 264 Andlau, famous for its convent, founded as early as the ninth century, where only daughters of the aristocracy were received, has a church whose wealth of carvings, especially on the portal in the porch, shows Lombard influence, frequently encountered here. Plate 263: frieze with elephant, griffin, hunting-leopards and lance-bearers. Plate 264: relief of Atlantids from the portal (after 1160).

265, 266 Throughout the Middle Ages Murbach—situated in the wooded valley of the river of that name—owned a great abbey, founded as early as the eighth century, which owed allegiance solely to the Emperor and the Pope. Of all its former splendour the imposing eastern part alone remains (Plate 266, second half twelfth century) with the lofty, twin-towered transept and the equally lofty flat choir wall (Cistercian influence), on which the Lombard decoration is quite distinct. The other ornamental carvings show the same peculiarity; for example, the tympanum on the portal of the south arm of the transept with its two isolated standing lions, its scroll-work and palmettes (Plate 265).

267-70 A typical Rhenish porch of Romanesque times can be seen between the two façade towers of the collegiate church of Lautenbach dedicated to St Michael and St Gangolph, although it was vaulted in the Gothic style at a later period. The many varied ornamental carvings, on the cubic capitals of the columns (Plates 268, 269) and in the left-hand frieze-like arrangement of capitals on the portal (Plate 270), constitute an excellent example of Romanesque sculpture in Alsace, expressed in a wealth of intertwining plant motifs and an imaginative treatment of animals and human beings—here representing various manifestations of sin (twelfth century).

271 The Abbey-Church of Ottmarsheim, little more than a mile from the Rhine, is a Carolingian octagonal building after the Aix pattern. Built in 1040 and consecrated in 1049, it shows that in the Empire the old imperial style of Romanesque art, bound by tradition, was still effective as late as the reign of the Salic Emperor Henry III, while the West, with its Romanized Franks liberated from the Empire, had already produced new forms.

BIBLIOGRAPHY

GENERAL:

Louis Bréhier, *Le Style roman*. Larousse, Paris, 1941.

Paul Deschamps, *Eglises romanes de France*. Didier, 1948.

Joan Evans, *Art in Medieval France, 987–1498*. Oxford University Press, 1948.

Joan Evans, *Cluniac Art of the Romanesque Period*. Cambridge University Press, 1950.

Henri Focillon, *Art d'Occident*. 3rd edition, Colin, Paris, 1955.

Louise Lefrançois-Pillion, *L'Art roman en France*. Le Prat, Paris.

Emile Mâle, *L'Art religieux du XIIe siècle en France*. 6th edition, Colin, Paris, 1953.

ARCHITECTURE:

Julius Baum, *Romanesque Architecture in France*. 2nd edition, Country Life, London, 1928.

Alfred W. Clapham, *Romanesque Architecture in Western Europe*. Clarendon Press, Oxford, 1936.

Joan Evans, *The Romanesque Architecture of the Order of Cluny*. Cambridge University Press, 1938.

Robert de Lasteyrie, *L'Architecture religieuse en France à l'époque romane*. 2nd edition, revised by Marcel Aubert. Picard, Paris, 1929.

Jean Vallery-Radot, *Eglises romanes. Filiations et échanges d'influences*. Renaissance du Livre, Paris, 1931.

SCULPTURE:

Marcel Aubert, *French Sculpture at the Beginning of the Gothic Period, 1140–1225*. Pantheon, Firenze; Pegasus Press, Paris, 1929.

Marcel Aubert, *La Sculpture française au moyen âge*. Flammarion, Paris, 1946.

Jurgis Baltrusaitis, *La Stylistique ornementale dans la sculpture romane*. Leroux, Paris, 1931.

Paul Deschamps, *French Sculpture of the Romanesque Period. Eleventh and Twelfth Centuries*. Pantheon, Firenze; Pegasus Press, Paris, 1930.

Paul Deschamps, *La Sculpture française. Epoque romane*. Edition du Chêne, Paris, 1947.

Henri Focillon, *L'Art des sculpteurs romans*. Leroux, Paris, 1931.

Arthur Gardner, *Medieval Sculpture in France*. Cambridge University Press, 1931.

Arthur Kingsley Porter, *Romanesque Sculpture of the Pilgrimage Roads*. Marshall Jones, Boston, 1923. The volumes dealing with France are as follows:

vol. I, Test; vol. II, Burgundy; vol. IV, Aquitaine; vol. VII, Western France; vol. VIII, Auvergne, Dauphine; vol. IX, Provence; vol. X, Ile-de-France.

WALL-PAINTING:

Edgar Waterman Anthony, *Romanesque Frescoes*. Princeton University Press, 1951.

Paul Deschamps and Marc Thibout, *La Peinture murale en France. Le haut moyen âge et l'époque romane*. Plon, Paris, 1951.

Henri Focillon, *Peintures romanes des églises de France*. Hartmann, Paris, 1950.

INDEX OF PLATES
ACCORDING TO PLACE NAMES

1 TOURNUS (Saône-et-Loire)

2 TOURNUS (Saône-et-Loire)

3 TOURNUS (Saône-et-Loire)

4 TOURNUS (Saône-et-Loire)

6 TOURNUS
(Saône-et-Loire)

7 TOURNUS (Saône-et-Loire)

8 FARGES (Saône-et-Loire)

9 TOURNUS (Saône-et-Loire)

10 TOURNUS (Saône-et-Loire)

11 CHAPAIZE (Saône-et-Loire)

13 CLUNY (Saône-et-Loire)

14 CLUNY (Saône-et-Loire)

15 CLUNY (Saône-et-Loire)

16 BERZÉ-LA-VILLE (Saône-et-Loire)

18 DIJON (Côte-d'Or)

19 AUTUN (Saône-et-Loire)

20   AUTUN (Saône-et-Loire)

21 AUTUN (Saône-et-Loire)

22 AUTUN (Saône-et-Loire)

23 AUTUN (Saône-et-Loire)

24 AUTUN (Saône-et-Loire)

25 MOUTIERS-ST-JEAN (Côte-d'Or)

26 SAULIEU (Côte-d'Or)

27 SAULIEU (Côte-d'Or)

28 AVALLON (Yonne)

29 AVALLON (Yonne)

31 VÉZELAY (Yonne)

32 VÉZELAY (Yonne)

33 VÉZELAY (Yonne)

34 VÉZELAY (Yonne)

35   DONZY-LE-PRÉ (Nièvre)

36 DONZY-LE-PRÉ (Nièvre)

40 NEVERS (Nièvre)

42 LA CHARITÉ-SUR-LOIRE (Nièvre)

43 LA CHARITÉ-SUR-LOIRE (Nièvre)

44 PARAY-LE-MONIAL (Saône-et-Loire)

45 PARAY-LE-MONIAL (Saône-et-Loire)

46 PARAY-LE-MONIAL (Saône-et-Loire)

47 MONTCEAU-L'ETOILE (Saône-et-Loire)

48 ANZY-LE-DUC (Saône-et-Loire)

49 ANZY-LE-DUC (Saône-et-Loire)

50 ANZY-LE-DUC (Saône-et-Loire)

51 ANZY-LE-DUC (Saône-et-Loire)

52 PERRECY-LES-FORGES (Saône-et-Loire)

54 NEUILLY-EN-DONJON (Allier)

55 SEMUR-EN-BRIONNAIS (Saône-et-Loire)

56 SEMUR-EN-BRIONNAIS (Saône-et-Loire)

57 CHARLIEU (Loire)

58✓59 CHARLIEU (Loire)

61 VIENNE (Isère)

62 ST-CHEF (Isère)

63 VION (Ardèche)

64 VION (Ardèche)

65 DIE (Drôme)

66 CRUAS (Ardèche)

67 CRUAS (Ardèche)

69 LA GARDE-ADHÉMAR (Drôme)

71 LE VAL DES NYMPHES (Drôme)

73 MANE (Basses-Alpes)

74 VAISON-LA-ROMAINE (Vaucluse)

76 SÉNANQUE (Vaucluse)

77 ST-TRINIT (Vaucluse)

78 ST-MICHEL-L'OBSERVATOIRE (BASSES-ALPES)

79 ST-MICHEL-L'OBSERVATOIRE (Basses-Alpes)

80 ST-CHRISTOL (Vaucluse)

81 SIMIANE (Basses-Alpes)

82 GANAGOBIE (Basses-Alpes)

83 EMBRUN (Hautes-Alpes)

84 MOUSTIERS-SAINTE-MARIE (Basses-Alpes)

85 LE THOR (Vaucluse)

86 ST-GABRIEL (Bouches-du-Rhône)

87 AVIGNON (Vaucluse)

88 MONTMAJOUR (Bouches-du-Rhône)

89 MONTMAJOUR (Bouches-du-Rhône)

93 AIX-EN-PROVENCE (Bouches-du-Rhône)

94 ST-GILLES-DU-GARD (Gard)

95 ST-GILLES-DU-GARD (Gard)

97 LES SAINTES-MARIES-DE-LA-MER (Bouches-du-Rhône)

98 ST-GUILHEM-LE-DESERT (Hérault)

99 TOULOUSE (Haute-Garonne)

101 TOULOUSE (Haute-Garonne)

106 TOULOUSE (Haute-Garonne)

107 ST-ANTONIN (Tarn-et-Garonne)

108 SERRABONE (Pyrénées-Orientales)

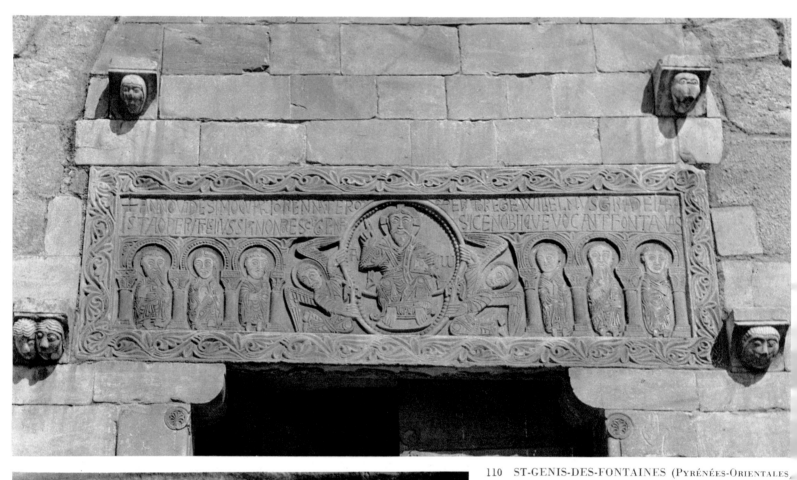

110   ST-GENIS-DES-FONTAINES (Pyrénées-Orientales

111   ST-GENIS-DES-FONTAINES (Pyrénées-Orientales)

112 ST-MARTIN-DU-CANIGOU (Pyrénées-Orientales)

113 ST-MICHEL-DE-CUXA (Pyrénées-Orientales)

114 ST-BERTRAND-DE-COMMINGES (Haute-Garonne)

115 ST-BERTRAND-DE-COMMINGES (Haute-Garonne)

117   OLORON-SAINTE-MARIE (Basses-Pyrénées)

119 OLORON-SAINTE-MARIE (Basses-Pyrénées)

120 MORLAAS (Basses-Pyrénées)

123 MOISSAC (Tarn-et-Garonne)

125 MOISSAC (Tarn-et-Garonne)

126 MOISSAC (Tarn-et-Garonne)

127 MOISSAC (Tarn-et-Garonne)

128 MOISSAC (Tarn-et-Garonne)

129 MOISSAC (Tarn-et-Garonne)

131 BEAULIEU-SUR-DORDOGNE (Corrèze)

132 BEAULIEU-SUR-DORDOGNE (Corrèze)

133 CARENNAC (Lot)

134 CONQUES (AVEYRON)

137 LE PUY (Haute-Loire)

139 LE PUY (Haute-Loire)

140 LE PUY (Haute-Loire)

141 LE PUY (Haute-Loire)

142 LE PUY (Haute-Loire)

143 YDES (Cantal)

144 BRIOUDE (Haute-Loire)

145 ST-NECTAIRE (Puy-de-Dôme)

146 ST-NECTAIRE (Puy-de-Dôme)

147 ISSOIRE (Puy-de-Dôme)

148 CHAMBON-SUR-LAC (Puy-de-Dôme)

149 ORCIVAL (Puy-de-Dôme)

150 BESSE-EN-CHANDESSE (Puy-de-Dôme)

151 BESSE-EN-CHANDESSE (Puy-de-Dôme)

152 BESSE-EN-CHANDESSE (Puy-de-Dôme)

153 MOZAC (Puy-de-Dôme)

154 CLERMONT-FERRAND (Puy-de-Dôme)

158　MARS-SUR-ALLIER (Nièvre)

159 MARS-SUR-ALLIER (Nièvre)

160 MARS-SUR-ALLIER (Nièvre)

161 BRINAY (Cher)

162 VICQ (INDRE)

163 VICQ (INDRE)

164 PLAIMPIED (Cher)

166　DÉOLS (Indre)

169 POITIERS (Vienne)

171 CIVRAY (Vienne)

173 CIVAUX (Vienne)

174 CIVAUX (Vienne)

175 CHARROUX (Vienne)

177 CHAUVIGNY (Vienne)

179 CHAUVIGNY (Vienne)

180 CHÂTEAU-LARCHER (Vienne)

181 ST-SAVIN (VIENNE)

183 ST-SAVIN (Vienne)

184 ST-SAVIN (Vienne)

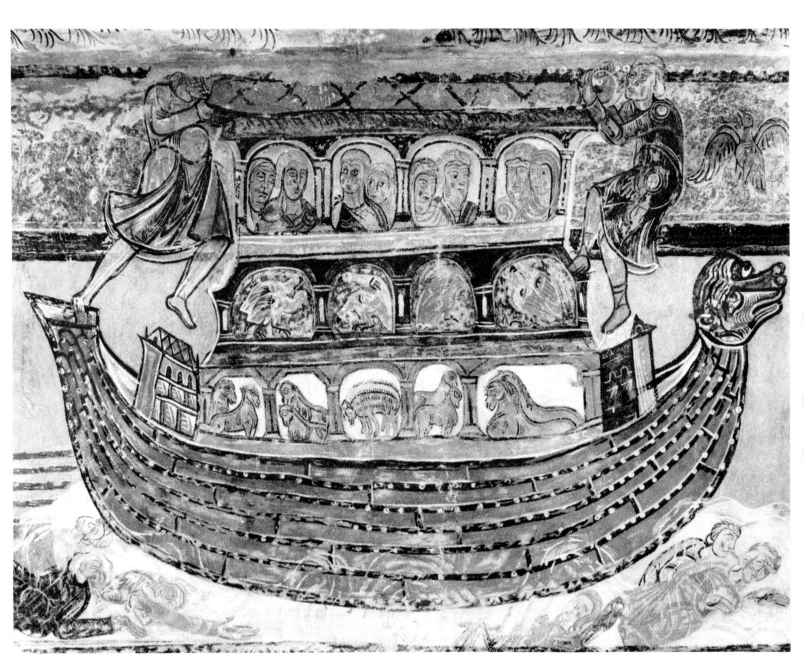

187 PÉRIGUEUX (Dordogne)

188 PÉRIGUEUX (Dordogne)

189 LICHÈRES (Charente)

190　ANGOULÊME (Charente)

192 SAINTES (Charente-Maritime)

193 RIOUX (Charente-Maritime)

194 AULNAY (Charente-Maritime)

195 AULNAY (Charente-Maritime)

196 ECHILLAIS (Charente-Maritime)

197 MELLE (Deux-Sèvres)

198 FENIOUX (Deux-Sèvres)

201 FOUSSAIS (Vendée)

203 PARTHENAY-LE-VIEUX (Deux-Sèvres)

204 ST-JOUIN-DE-MARNES (Deux-Sèvres)

205　ST-JOUIN-DE-MARNES (Deux-Sèvres)

207 THOUARS (Deux-Sèvres)

209 LAVARDIN (Loir-et-Cher)

208 TAVANT (Indre-et-Loire)

210 AZAY-LE-RIDEAU (INDRE-ET-LOIRE)

213 AREINES (Loir-et-Cher)

216 CHARTRES (Eure-et-Loir)

217 CHARTRES (Eure-et-Loir)

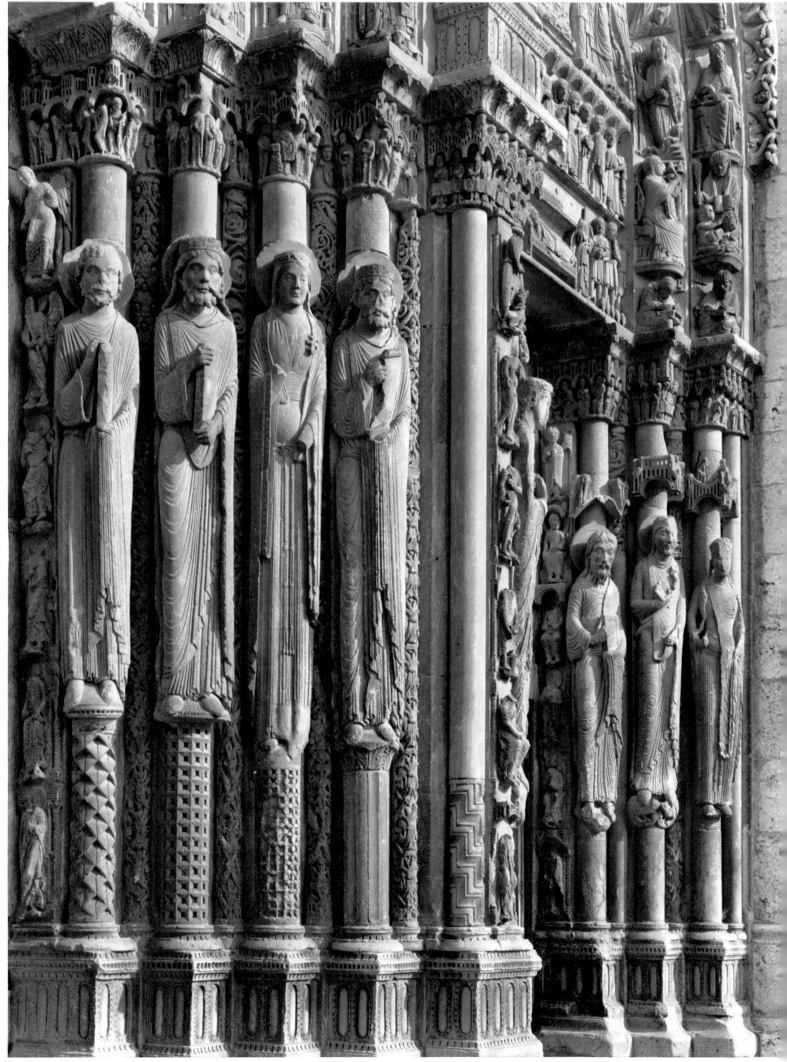

221 ETAMPES (Seine-et-Oise)

222 BOURGES (Cher)

224 ST-BENOÎT-SUR-LOIRE (LOIRET)

225 ST-BENOÎT-SUR-LOIRE (Loiret)

226 ST-BENOÎT-SUR-LOIRE (Loiret)

227 ST-BENOÎT-SUR-LOIRE (Loiret)

228 ST-BENOÎT-SUR-LOIRE (Loiret)

229 ST-BENOÎT-SUR-LOIRE (Loiret)

230 ST-BENOÎT-SUR-LOIRE (Loiret)

231 GERMIGNY-LES-PRÉS (Loiret)

232 ST-LOUP-DE-NAUD (Seine-et-Marne)

233 PROVINS (Seine-et-Marne)

235 MORIENVAL (OISE)

236 MORIENVAL (Oise)

237 SOISSONS (Aisne)

238 SOISSONS (Aisne)

239 BRAISNE (Aisne)

241 LAON (Aisne)

242 · NOUVION-LE-VINEUX (AISNE)

243 REIMS (Marne)

244 REIMS (Marne)

245 REIMS (Marne)

246 REIMS (Marne)

247 MONT ST-MICHEL (Manche)

248 MONT ST-MICHEL (Manche)

249 CAEN (Calvados)

250 CAEN (Calvados)

252 CAEN (Calvados)

253 CAEN (Calvados)

254 THAON (Calvados)

255 BAYEUX (Calvados)

256 JUMIÈGES (Seine-Maritime)

257 ST-MARTIN-DE-BOSCHERVILLE (Seine-Maritime)

258 LE MANS (Sarthe)

259 LE MANS (Sarthe)

261 POMPIERRE (Vosges)

262 SÉLESTAT (Bas-Rhin)

263 ANDLAU (Bas-Rhin)

264 ANDLAU (Bas-Rhin)

265 MURBACH (Haut-Rhin)

266 MURBACH (Haut-Rhin)

268 LAUTENBACH (Haut-Rhin)

269 LAUTENBACH (Haut-Rhin)

270 LAUTENBACH (Haut-Rhin)

271 OTTMARSHEIM (Haut-Rhin)